Prayer Like Great Drops Of Blood
Falling Down To The Ground

PRAYER LIKE GREAT DROPS OF BLOOD FALLING DOWN TO THE GROUND

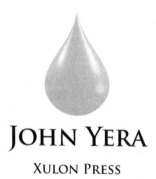

JOHN YERA

XULON PRESS

Xulon Press
2301 Lucien Way #415
Maitland, FL 32751
407.339.4217
www.xulonpress.com

Scripture quotations taken from the English Standard
Version (ESV). Copyright © 2001 by Crossway, a
publishing ministry of Good News Publishers. Used by
permission. All rights reserved.

Printed in the United States of America.

ISBN-13: 9781545622070

PRAYER

"LIKE GREAT DROPS OF
BLOOD FALLING DOWN TO
THE GROUND"

LUKE 22:39-46

BY:
PASTOR JOHN YERA

Foreword

⸺◦⟨✧⟩◦⸺

In Philippians 4:6-7, the Apostle Paul, writing under the inspiration of the Holy Spirit, reminds us: *"Do not be anxious about anything, **but in every situation, by prayer and petition,** with thanksgiving, present your requests to God. And the peace of God, which transcends all understanding, will guard your hearts and your minds in Christ Jesus."*

My brother in Christ, friend, and fellow minister of the Gospel, John Yera, has written a powerful primer on prayer. With fidelity to and reliance upon the Scriptures, the Holy Spirit's guidance, and his own life experiences, John has written about the most important ingredient for living an effective and joyful Christian life: becoming a person of prayer.

Why should we pray? How do we pray? What difference can prayer make? John's booklet on prayer gives scriptural answers to these questions and more. But most importantly, it challenges us to stop just talking about prayer and start praying. This is a motivational book to get us into the habit of regular and continuous prayer.

This booklet should be read with an open Bible. There are countless verses to meditate upon and study more fully. Unlike a novel, it's intent is not to be read through at one sitting, but to be used as a regular study aid and motivational prayer guide during one's times of personal worship and meditation.

John regularly echoes the question in his own words which Corrie ten Boom used to challenge Christians of an earlier genera-tion: *"Is prayer your steering wheel or your spare tire?"* He encourages us to stop living lives that are spiritually powerless and filled with worry and anxiety. His call is to a pow-er-filled life of prayer and praise.

As his former pastor, I can personally verify that John practices what he preaches. **He is a man of prayer.** Faced with paralysis that limits his body to a wheelchair, his soul soars on the winds of the Holy Spirit as he prays. The example of His life is as inspirational as his writings on prayer.

I commend this booklet to all Christians. The weakness of our spiritual lives and the weakness of our churches all rest on our lack of prayer. In a troubled time like our day, prayer is especially needed. I challenge you to hear John's words and the voice of the Holy Spirit calling you to become a woman or a man of prayer.

Reverend Alan Stanford, Ph.D.

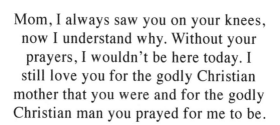

Mom, I always saw you on your knees, now I understand why. Without your prayers, I wouldn't be here today. I still love you for the godly Christian mother that you were and for the godly Christian man you prayed for me to be.

Reiff, you were my pastor, my teacher, my mentor, and my friend. I will never forget you. I am the pastor, the teacher, the mentor, and the friend to so many thanks to you. Our times of prayer together, even in your last days, I will never forget. That special time of prayer with you made me who I am today.

TABLE OF CONTENTS

—⧓—

Jesus Prays on the Mount of Olives (Luke 22:39-46)

———⟨∘⟨𝒮⟩∘⟩———

³⁹ And he came out and went, as was his custom, to the Mount of Olives, and the disciples followed him. ⁴⁰ And when he came to the place, he said to them, "Pray that you may not enter into temptation." ⁴¹ And he withdrew from them about a stone's throw, and knelt down and prayed, ⁴² saying, "Father, if you are willing, remove this cup from me. Nevertheless, not my will, but yours, be done." ⁴³ And there appeared to him an angel from heaven, strengthening him. ⁴⁴ And being in agony he prayed more earnestly; **and his sweat became like great drops of blood falling down to the ground.** ⁴⁵ And when he rose from prayer, he came to the disciples and found them

sleeping for sorrow, [46] and he said to them, "Why are you sleeping? Rise and pray that you may not enter into temptation."[1]

---

[1] Unless otherwise indicated, all scripture quotations are taken from The Holy Bible: English Standard Version. (2016). Wheaton, IL: Crossway Bibles.

Introduction

———◇·◦⟨◎⟩◦·◇———

I know many people, Christians and non-believers alike, wonder if prayer works. I use the word "works" because ultimately, when we pray, we are coming before God with some petition or request, as I did the day I got shot in the line-of-duty. When that bullet hit my spine, I did not have time to think of any earthly matters, just barely thinking of the ones I love. I did not feel at that moment I had the luxury to think of too many things with perhaps a fraction of a second to live as that bullet shattered my spine, feeling like a thousand volts of electricity coursing through my body, numbing me instantly. It is amazing that at that moment, money, possessions, things, concerns, my job—the clutter of our daily lives—just did not seem important when I felt like I was about to die. I had but a fraction of a millisecond to think, *I don't want to die*.

I can say with certainty now as a dedicated follower of Jesus Christ that I know what it feels like to meet death head-on, not knowing the eternal consequences when not walking in the presence of the Lord. Although I grew up going to church, "religious" things such as prayer or being "in the Word" were not a priority in my life. Everything appeared to be going well. I was married to a gorgeous woman. I had two beautiful healthy kids, an exciting job, and my thought at the time was, God was something or someone I reverenced in a way, but I kept Him in the background. What was important was, "I have made it, I'm doing good, and all of *my* hard work had paid off!" It was all about what *I* did, what *I* achieved, what *I* have, never giving God any credit for what *He* has done, what *He* has given *me*, for the very life *I* have because of *Him*.

Well, I arrived at the day in my life rather suddenly when the realization hit me like a bolt of lightning that it was not about *me* or what *I* can do, but about God and what *He* can do and had done all throughout my life.

My one simple but brief prayer to Him at that frightful moment in my life when that bullet shattered my spine, threatening to cut my life short was, *"God, please do not let me die!"* Working as an undercover narcotics agent, I often found myself in some harrowing situations, on an occasion or two staring down the barrel of a gun, and suddenly, it was time to reach out to my Creator, whom I had ignored for so long, and ask, but in a fraction of a second, for His mercy. Those were the only words I remember saying that day, whether out loud or in my mind, before I fell to the ground and total darkness encompassed me.

I came to consciousness a while later; seconds or minutes did not seem relevant. Nothing was important other than I knew I was alive because I heard the voice of someone near me saying, "John, you're going to be okay." They may have been lying to me, just saying comforting words to me because somehow, I felt and knew I was paralyzed, yet all I remember was the sheer excitement in the inner being of my soul that I was alive.

As time goes by and I think of those words I prayed, of how I cried out to God to let me live; and He did! I have thanked

Him every day since for giving me a second chance at life. I believe that was the shortest prayer in my entire life, but I am also convinced the answer to that prayer has affected me profoundly ever since. I was given a second chance at a life I never would have experienced had I not gone to Him in prayer that fateful day I got shot. Of that, I am eternally convinced!

I have lived a life full of praise and joy since, as I serve Him with gladness each day, and, the more I think about it, the more I believe it was not so much that I did not want to die that day, but that He wanted me to live! God gave me that chance to live life and live it abundantly,[2] not that I may continue to accumulate things or accomplish and perform and take all the credit for what *I* can do, but to ultimately give *Him* the credit, honor, and glory due to Him for all He has done and continues to do in my life.

Jesus said the destructive scheme of the devil is to steal, kill, and to destroy[3] all that we can have in the faithful care of our Good Shepherd Jesus Christ, and, it is until we decide whom we will serve and

---

[2] John 10:10.

[3] Ibid.

acknowledge who will faithfully save us that we can then decide whether we truly want to live or die. The road to this life with Christ without a doubt is not an easy one as Jesus said, "Enter through the narrow gate. For wide is the gate and broad is the road that leads to destruction, and many enter through it. But small is the gate and narrow the road that leads to life, and only a few find it." (Matthew 7:13-14)

No doubt this narrow gate leads to a hard road—in fact, it may very well be one of sorrow and suffering, but, if in the process of traveling this road, one should lose one's life, one would truly find a better one than what this life here on earth can offer.[4] The hardships and difficult decisions we will make along this road are what will lead to salvation and eternal life to everyone who accepts it. (John 1:12, 3:16-18; Romans 10:9; 1 John 2:2)

My prayer for life, for salvation that fateful day I was shot, was to God, the only One who can provide us the path to eternal life. (Romans 5:6-8) I made my choice that day, knowing from where my life came (John 1:3-4) and to where I wanted it to go

---

[4] Matthew 16:25; Luke 9:24; Mark 8:35.

for the remainder of my days and into eternity, "For with you is the fountain of life." (Psalm 36:9) Remember, the devil is the great deceiver and will make you believe accumulating more stuff is truly living, and that without all he offers, life is not worth living. What the devil is ultimately doing at the end is taking our very lives in return for what he has given us: "For what will it profit a man if he gains the whole world and forfeits his soul?" (Matthew 16:26; Mark 8:36; Luke 12:20)

Such was the life of the rich man in the parable told by Jesus, (Luke 12:13-21) who was consumed with all he had, wanting more, saving more, believing he had all he could possibly need or want, yet Jesus made it clear that the man was foolish. You "fool" (Luke 12:20) Jesus said to him, reminding him he would die that night and all he had would just go to someone else to enjoy. Jesus says the love of money or wealth is vanity, meaning it is futile, meaningless. "He who loves money will not be satisfied with money, nor he who loves wealth with his income; this also is vanity." (Ecclesiastes 5:10) What, then, is it all about, you ask? What is the meaning of life? What are we here for? The Bible clearly answers all these questions and many more by telling us it is this simple: "Fear God and keep His commandments, for this is the whole duty of man." (Ecclesiastes 12:13) Everything else is vanity!

So then, why do we pray? Well, we certainly don't pray to impress or inform God; for what can we tell Him He does not know or has not done since the beginning of time and even before that? God is omnipotent, omnipresent, and omniscient; God is sovereign over it all. "God is greater than our heart, and He knows everything." (1 John 3:20) My simple answer to this question is, we pray that His will be done, (Matthew 6:10b) that no matter what we are on our knees for, that whatever we do ask for, He will receive all the glory! Such a simple answer, but I would not have arrived at this conclusion had it not been for (1 Corinthians 10:31) which says, "So, whether you eat or drink, or whatever you do, do all to the glory of God."

Do we work, collect, hoard, and get more and more in this life all for the glory of God or for our personal satisfaction? Jesus, our prime example of what it means to give God the glory, was not rich or famous or popular as the world would define those terms, but was made low, poor, and humble, "By becoming obedient to the point of death, even death on a cross." (Philippians 2:8) It was because of this unswerving obedience to His Father in Heaven that God "Bestowed on Him the name that is above every name, so that at the name of Jesus every knee should bow, in Heaven and on earth and under the earth, and every tongue confess that Jesus Christ is Lord, to the glory of God the Father." (Philippians 2:9-11)

That is why we pray; that is why Jesus prayed in His high priestly prayer in John 17:5, "And now, Father, glorify me in your own presence with the glory that I had with you before the world existed." That is why I prayed that fateful day, unbeknownst to me that indeed, God would receive the glory for saving me, not only to live a little longer, but into eternity. Jesus gave life to Lazarus, (John 11) all for the glory of God, (John 11:4) all so that when we pray about something, we may believe God will answer and He will receive the glory He deserves. "Commit your way to the Lord; trust in Him, and He will act." (Psalm 37:5)

The beauty of prayer is that when we don't know what it is we ought to pray for, God's Holy Spirit, which lives within each of us who has received Him as Savior and Lord in our lives, helps us in our weaknesses, in our frailties, in our physical, emotional, and spiritual disabilities.[5] It is the Holy Spirit, God Himself, who helps us in our times of need and distress.

My daughter asked me one day, "Dad, if Jesus was praying to His Father while in the garden of Gethsemane, and He Himself is God, then you are telling me Jesus was praying to Himself?" The thought provoking words from the mouths of babes! The only way I could answer her was, "Yes, Jesus being God was indeed praying to God the Father, as if to say, the only way to God is through God Himself." (John 14:6) The Father, the Son, and the Holy Spirit are divine persons that live in perfect harmony and are indeed worthy of our praise, worship, and prayers. As you pray then, know you are praying to the Father, through the Son, in the power and presence of the Holy Spirit that lives in you. Jesus tells us, "Whatever you ask in my name, this I will do, that the Father may be glorified in the Son. If you ask me anything in my name, I will do it." (John 14:13-14) It is through Christ that we

---

[5] Romans 8:27.

can have access to the Father, and it is in the power of the Spirit who "Intercedes for us with groans too deep for words," (Romans 8:26) that we pray to the Father, for as the Spirit intercedes on our behalf, God knows what the Spirit is thinking and Christ Jesus, who is at the right hand of God, is indeed also interceding for us. (Rom. 8:34)

One important thing to remember about the Holy Trinity when we are in prayer is that where one member of the Trinity is present, the others are as well. "For where two or three are gathered in my name, there am I among them." (Matthew 18:20) So, when you pray, know with every fiber of your being that the Father, Son, and Holy Spirit hear your prayers and respond as one. It is such an awesome feeling to know, and to honor the role each member of the Godhead has in our lives as believers that where two or three would agree together about anything, it would be done for them by the Father in Heaven.

Ultimately, when we do pray, it is God's own passion and desire that we glorify Him, as He zealously says, "My glory I will not give to another." (Isaiah 48:11) And, it is not that we choose to give Him glory, because, for that reason, He chose us before the foundation of the world, that we would be blameless and holy before Him as we give Him the glory and honor He deserves from us. That is the very reason "He, in love, predestined us to adoption as sons through Jesus Christ to Himself." "All to the praise of His glory!" (Ephesians 1:4-6, 13-14)

Therefore, we must ask ourselves every day, "Is what I am saying and doing and praying all for His glory?" It must make us think every moment of the day, how then can I believe in Him, when all I do is receive glory from others because of what I say and do, yet I do not seek the glory that comes from the only God. (John 5:44) As we get on our knees every day, we must be mindful as we pray in Jesus' name that it is not about what we want, but ultimately what God wants so that He may be glorified. "Whatever you ask in my name, this I will do, that the Father may be glorified in the Son." (John 14:13) That is the joy of my serving Him: that in all I do, God may be glorified!

I have seen and experienced much joy in my life since the day He saved me. God has answered so many prayers, not only in my life, but in the lives of so many others I have prayed for and with, that it is enough to convince me prayer works. It was a privilege for me to be a member of the pastor search committee at my church and before we even started the arduous task of searching and selecting the candidate the church would then vote on, our group prayed for the weeks and months of long hours that lay ahead of us. I wrote an article in the Leesburg Community Church newsletter with the intention of spurring on the church to pray and be a part of this most important work on which we were embarking. Toward the end of the search, as we had narrowed the candidate from three, to two, and then finally to one, I personally started feeling a little anxious. Questions and doubts started clouding my thoughts. *"What if he is not the right one we are choosing?"* *"What will happen if he is the wrong one?"* *"Will I be blamed?"* I was in fact second-guessing myself until I remembered and re-read the prayer article I had written before the search even began: "Only Through Prayer."[6] What an encouragement to realize we simply could not pick the wrong person because we had already put the search, the selection, the whole process

6   Yera, John. "Only Through Prayer" Leesburgcc.org, last modified November 22, 2016, http://leesburgcc.org/uploads/november_2016.pdf.

in God's hands through prayer. It was He who had already ordained and chosen our pastor, "I have called you by name, you are mine." (Isaiah 43:1c) A relief rushed through me when the second-guessing was over for at that moment I knew it all happened "only through prayer." (Mark 9:29)

So, next time you may feel inclined to ask, "Why pray?" Perhaps the question that you should be asking yourself instead is, "Why breathe?" For just as breathing is essential to our physical well-being, so is prayer crucial to the well-being of our soul.

"Pray then like this." (Matthew 6:9) As Martin Luther, the religious reformer of the sixteenth century Protestant Reformation so eloquently said, "To be a Christian without praying is no more possible than to be alive without breathing." To Him be glory forever and ever. (1 Peter 4:11; Romans 11:36) May "The grace of the Lord Jesus be with all…" (Revelation 22:21) as you embark on your personal journey of prayer.

Chapter 1

Jesus Prayed as Was His Custom (Luke 22:39)

"*And he came out and went, as was his custom, to the Mount of Olives, and the disciples followed him.*" (Luke 22:39)[7] The night before His crucifixion, Jesus went to the Garden of Gethsemane on the Mount of Olives to pray as was His custom, as He so often did,[8] and His disciples followed Him, as they had been doing so for the last few years of Jesus' life and especially since He uttered those life changing words to them, "*Follow me.*" (Matthew 4:19; 16:24) We know this was indeed His custom to pray because "*Everyday He was teaching*

[7] Luke 22:39-46; Matthew 26:30; Mark 14:26; John 18:1.

[8] Matthew 21:1; Mark 14:26; John 18:1-2; Luke 2:37.

in the temple, but at night He went out and lodged on the mount called Olivet." (Luke 21:37) This made it easy for Judas to betray Him, for this disloyal follower was but a few of the privileged inner circle of Jesus that knew this is where Jesus often would be found praying with His disciples. (John 18:2) Knowing Judas' heart, Jesus could have easily moved to another place to pray, but why try to evade what must happen according to Scripture as written prophetically so long before that night in the garden. (Zechariah 11:13; Matt. 27: 9)

"*Even my close friend, someone I trusted, one who shared my bread, has turned against me.*" (Psalm 41:9) Though we may want to focus on the reason Jesus went to the garden in the first place, which was to pray, we cannot, however, overlook the agony, the treason, the treachery that was about to unfold for all history to record and for all humanity to wallow in its culpability, complicit via our sins. For what was about to take place, even His disciples could not have even imagined. "But God demonstrates His love for us in that while we were still sinners, Christ died for us." (Romans 5:8)

How is it that so many people were out to kill Jesus, yet so few knew where

He could be found? How that speaks volumes about prayer that only those closest to Him would know where to find Him, be it early in the morning, (Mark 1:35) or while it was still dark. This should be where we ought to be found by those that know us best: on our knees in the most of privileged places that only those intimately close to us and our Father would know to find. We discover Jesus most often on His knees before His Heavenly Father, and we would hope others would find us by His side, on our knees in our own times of consuming grief that this world is but most happy to heap on us. Prayer must be one habit we would want to pattern after our teacher and have a strong need for, withdrawing to lonely places to pray, (Luke 5:16) to be alone with our Father in Heaven, seeking His divine guidance and instructions for our lives.

As Psalm 25:9 would comfort us, "*He leads the humble in what is right, and teaches the humble His way.*" What better assurance is there to know that we are in the center of His will for our lives and that in prayer we are daily under His protection, (Psalm 23, 25, 71, 91:14) as we are daily surrounded by those not only willing to betray us, but send us to our death believing they are "Offering service to God." (John 16:2) Especially as we "See the Day drawing near." (Hebrews 10:25), the habit of prayer should become more fervent, never giving up . Our mutual efforts in prayer are crucial for "The coming of the Lord is at hand." (Zephaniah 1:14; James 5:8; 1 Peter 4:7; Rom. 13:11, 12; Phil. 4:5; He. 10:25, 37) We must maintain a steadfast hope in Him and not be tempted to defect from our professions of faith in Christ "For He who calls you is faithful." (1 Thessalonians 5:24) "He who began a good work in you will bring it to completion at the day of Jesus Christ." (Philippians 1:6)

Jesus knew He had to withdraw to lonely quiet places to pray, otherwise the demands of the day would have left Him spiritually devoid, lost, weak, and most fatally, without the guidance, strength, and protection of His Father in Heaven. As a man, Jesus knew He would be vulnerable. We need to heed this advice daily lest we start to believe we can accomplish things on our own power. Not long after His baptism, Satan tempted Jesus,[9] and as His ministry began, we see Jesus immediately healing a man with an unclean spirit, rebuking and casting out

---

[9] Matthew 3:13-17; 4:1-11, Mark 1:9-11; Luke 3:21, 22; John 1:32-34.

demons and, healing many. (Mark 1:21-31; Matthew 8:14-15; Luke 4:38-39) This would seem to us as just another day on the job for Jesus, after all, He is the Son of God; but as you read this fast-paced account of all He did, we don't see God Himself in action, but a man that no doubt was God, yet who took on a fleshly body. (John 1:14) Jesus never relinquished His status as God, (John 1:1, 14) yet He became fully human. (Hebrews 2:17) For our sake, He would know what it meant to go to bed exhausted as we see Him sleeping in a boat, (Mark 4:38) or thirsty and exhausted, (John 4:6) even experiencing the human emotion of grief as He shed a tear for His friend Lazarus. (John 11:35) The only and most important difference is that although human in every way, He never stopped being God, He never sinned, (Hebrews 4:15) remaining perfect in every way for, "*It was fitting God … should make the author of salvation perfect through suffering.*" (Hebrews 2:10)

For all that He did, He knew that in His first actions in ministry, He was not going to be able to do anything on His own. We see that very dependence on God and His Word while in the wilderness being tempted by the devil, able only to withstand the assaults of the evil one by knowing exactly what it is; the infallible and inerrant Word of God says; *"It is written."* (Luke 4:8,10; Ephesians 6:17)

That is why the next morning, before He went to preach in Galilee, Jesus, *"Rising very early in the morning, while it was still dark, He departed and went out to a desolate place, and there He prayed."* (Mark 1:35; Luke 5:16; Matthew 14:23) Based on all He had done the day before, Jesus knew it wasn't going to get easier. Satan was not going to let up on tempting Him just because He is the Son of God, instead, "Opting to wait until an opportune time." (Luke 4:13), lying in wait, "Like a roaring lion, seeking someone to devour." (1 Peter 5:8)

Though with His mere presence, Jesus, is able to instill terror in demons as they cry out to Him, *"I know who you are -- the Holy One of God."* (Mark 1:24), the devil and his minions are relentless in their pursuit of separating us from our fellowship and worship of God as he so audaciously tried separating the Son from the love of the Father. Should we neglect to be on our knees, we are but vulnerable, lost, and defenseless sheep. Jesus says, *"Behold, I am sending you out as sheep in the midst of wolves, so be wise as serpents and innocent as doves."*

(Matthew 10:16) Our ministries, in the midst of an unfriendly world requires that we be prepared to face the hostilities and attacks certain to come our way, "*For we do not wrestle against flesh and blood, but against the rulers, against the authorities, against the cosmic powers over this present darkness, against the spiritual forces of evil in the heavenly places.*" (Ephesians 6:12)

What better way to combat this spiritual warfare than to be on our knees as our Savior and Lord taught us? Jesus knew early in His earthly ministry how vital prayer was for guidance, wisdom, strength, and protection from God. Jesus' ministry for which He came; preaching "repentance and forgiveness." (Luke 24:47) "To seek and to save the lost." (Luke 19:10), would not fail, as "*He is able to save to the uttermost those who draw near to God through him, since he always lives to make intercession for them.*" (Hebrews 7:25) Though the shadow of the cross loomed near, He would be victorious, for He knew, "*This is the will of Him who sent me, that I should lose nothing of all that He has given me, but raise it up on the last day.*" (John 6:39) What a glorious assurance for us to know, "*Everyone who looks on the*

Son and believes in Him should have eternal life." (John 6:40)

When Jesus said, "Follow me"[10] this meant picking up your own cross and following Him to where He was headed and where, so many have turned around and still do, rejecting this offer, (John 6:66) for to truly follow Him means to deny oneself and follow nothing or no one but Him. (Luke 9:23) To follow Him means understanding and knowing that to do so, it cannot be done by sheer human strength or willpower. It is only through God's Spirit (John 6:63) that we will find the strength to not only observe and participate, but to do all He did, "And greater works than these will he do." (John 14:12) We are to pray as we ought, though we may not have the words. (Romans 8:26) God's Spirit will help us in our weakness not only for now, but forever. (John 14:16)

We are commanded in Scriptures to "Pray without ceasing." (1 Thessalonians 5:17) Not that we may become weary in the process, but that we may rejoice more as we maintain continuous fellowship with God during our daily struggles, having not our concentration and communication

---

[10] Matthew 8:22; 9:9; Mark 2:14; Luke 5:27; John 1:43.

with God hindered in any way, lest we miss out on seeing Him work as we labor on our knees. Will there be daily distractions as the flaming darts of the evil one (Ephesians 6:16) relentlessly come our way each waking moment of our lives so that we may either give up praying or put it off, sometimes indefinitely? Let this not happen, God forbid, as Jesus warns us to be ready at all times, not just sometimes, not just occasionally, as He reminds us, "But stay awake at all times, praying that you may have strength to escape all these things that are going to take place, and to stand before the Son of Man." (Luke 21:36)[11] Oh Lord, how I pray that our hearts are truly committed to you, that as we make it our custom to pray, nothing can stand between us and full communion with you.

---

[11] Romans 12:12; Ephesians 6:18; Colossians 4:2; 1; Thess. 5:17.

CHAPTER 2

Pray That You May Not Enter Into Temptation (Luke 22:40)

————— ∞◦❦◦∞ —————

"And when he came to the place, he said to them, 'Pray that you may not enter into temptation.'" (Luke 22:40) If anyone knew what it meant to be tempted, it was Jesus. Satan tempted Him in the wilderness for forty days and when not successful in his temptation, the devil didn't just give up, leaving Him not permanently, but, "Until an opportune time." (Luke 4:13, 22:53; John 14:30) The Bible has made it abundantly clear that the devil is the "god of this world." (2 Corinthians 4:4) "prince of the power of the air." (Ephesians 2:2) The "ruler of this world." (John 14:30) And, as a result, he has a major influence on a great number of people and their thoughts, desires, and hopes. The sad thing, if not scary, is that if he has the audacity to try to encourage the Son of God to fall into temptation and sin, so can he boldly attempt to influence us in such subtle ways that we may not even be aware we are being led toward evil. The devil is the father of lies and deceptions, but Jesus showed the devil and his wily schemes, that though He was fully man and subject to the same temptations as us, He was, is, and always will be the living Son of God and, as a result, He could not be tempted no matter what the devil offered Him. Jesus is God incarnate and so James 1:13 tells us, "God cannot be tempted with evil, and He Himself tempts no one."

Jesus was emptied of His divine prerogatives, (Philippians 2:7) leaving Him just as vulnerable as any fleshly being. Yet, though His complete and absolute deity was put aside that He may fully embrace His perfect sinless humanity, (Hebrews 4:15) all that He may share in our own frailties, He remained Holy and unblemished; even the demons knew "He was the Holy One of God." (Mark 1:24) The devil may have wished to imprison Jesus with all his offers of power, fame, and fortune as he subjects so many of us successfully, but thanks be to God, Jesus Christ was crucified and resurrected as the living Son of God. He resisted any offer the devil could make to Him so that we may also know what it is to truly live a life in Christ, free of bondage to sin and the evil one. (John 8:32)

It is no wonder that the very first thing Jesus tells His disciples upon entering the garden to do was, "Watch and pray that you may not enter into temptation. The spirit indeed is willing, but the flesh is weak." (Matthew 26:41) Did they fully comprehend this admonition to "Be self-controlled and sober-minded for the sake of your prayers." (1 Peter 4:7) How else is there for Christians to pray, but with a clear mind, a sound mind, that we may fully appreciate through prayer, "The grace that will be brought to you at the revelation of Jesus Christ." (1 Peter 1:13) How else but on our knees, will we have the fortitude to bear and "Escape all these things that are going to take place." (Luke 21:36)

Jesus says, "Submit yourselves therefore to God. Resist the devil, and he will flee from you." (James 4:7) This is our commitment as Christians, not to give our adversary the opportunity to draw us away from

prayer, but resist him, standing firm in our
faith and resolve that at the end of the day,
in the strength and might of the Lord, we
hold firmly to all that we have victoriously
conquered in His mighty powerful name;
our churches, our people, our families, our
homes, our nation. It is a matter of eternal
life and eternal death and while we have
breath in our lungs, we must make the best
use of the time we have on bended knees,
"Because the days are evil." (Ephesians
6:13) The only way to be able to withstand
is by "Praying, at all times in the Spirit."
(Ephesians 6:18) The only way we are going
to survive as we are warned in Scripture is
to "Be on guard, keep awake. For you do
not know when the time will come." (Mark
13:33) When Jesus repeatedly cautions us
to, be on guard, be alert, and be constantly
awake, it is because He desires us as His
servants to be mindful and vigilant to all the
spiritual dangers and traps that lay before us
just waiting to pounce on us and "Devour us
like a roaring lion." (1 Peter 5:8)

Christ says, "But exhort one another as
long as it is called 'today' that none of you
may be hardened by the deceitfulness of sin."
(Hebrews 3:13) No wonder Jesus warned
His disciples not to fall into temptation, for

He knew of the clear and present danger of the temptation of sin that can and has seeped into our lives, homes, and even churches. How this deceitfulness of sin can lure us away and deceive us, even those that are indwelt with the power of the Holy Spirit, if that is possible. (Matthew 24:24)

No sooner did Jesus arrive at the garden to pray that He urged—in fact, insisted—that His disciples immediately *"Pray that they may not enter into temptation."* (Luke 22:40), for He knew one of them had already indeed succumbed to that temptation soon to betray his Master. As Scripture itself spoke about it prophetically so long before, "Even my close friend in whom I trusted, who ate my bread, has lifted his heel against me." (Psalm 41:9; John 13:18; Matt. 26:23) Jesus exhorted His disciples to pray, for He knew of the horrific trials and tribulations that were coming His way, and soon their way and, ultimately, our way. The temptations from the devil are all meant to hinder or stop us all together from praying and so the great things we may or could accomplish through prayer would no longer be, ultimately denying God the glory He deserves.

Jesus knew, therefore He prayed, and therefore He did everything so excellently, that the Son may glorify His Father in all He does. (John 17:1) When we do the opposite of what we are to do, that is not walking in holy obedience to God, then it is Satan who receives the glory and not our Lord. As the Son said, "I glorified you on earth, having accomplished the work that you gave me to do." (John 17:4) So then, must we make it our preeminent goal in this life to be in unity with our Lord for "The glory that you have given me I have given to them, that they may be one even as we are one." (John 17:22)

Many a Christian today has rejected the doctrine of Truth of God and in order that they may be as inclusive and tolerant as possible within the church; accommodation, and compromise has taken over and so many of us live according to the world's standards neglecting to even pray, hence, missing the mark of God's standards and of God's glory. (Romans 3:23) Sin, simply put, is lawlessness, (1 John 3:4) so when we neglect or refuse to pray as we ought, we are saying, "I don't care about you God. I don't care about who you are, and what you want, or what you say is truth."

"Pray that you may not enter into temptation." (Luke 22:40) Jesus cried this out to His disciples, for soon they would know the power of God's truth, that will indeed reveal how He, standing right before them was the "Lamb of God who takes away the sin of the world." (John 1:29) That He would show people from "Every tribe and language and people and nation." (Revelation 5:9), that He is indeed God incarnate and that only through Him can anyone know "The way, the truth and the life." (John 14:6) And, that "No one comes to the Father except through me." (John 14:6)

Sin does indeed have the power to enslave us, which is evident in the lives of unbelievers and, in the way they live, accountable to no one, for instead they have chosen to be under the power of the dominion of sin. But for us, those whom "He gave the right to become children of God." (John 1:12), our lives are different because of the power of Christ. "For we know that our old self was crucified with Him so that the body ruled by sin might be done away with, that we should no longer be slaves to sin." (Romans 6:6) That is perhaps the message Jesus was conveying to His disciples when they first entered that garden to pray, that they not enter into temptation, that they understand that in Him they are no longer slaves to sin, but are now slaves of Jesus! Even in the garden, the only choice the disciples had was to pray; or not, there was no middle ground. Either you are yoked with Jesus in prayer or yoked with the world in sin. Either you are "Cold or hot." (Revelation 3:15), but not lukewarm because all that would leave us is spiritually bankrupt, wretched, pitiful, poor, blind, and readily even unaware of the temptation that will befall us as we sleep instead of pray.

When Jonah was called by God to go to Nineveh, (Jonah 1:1) Jonah instead decided to disobey God's call and, so he jumped on a ship to take him away from what God had appointed him to do. As we know, God is always sovereignly in control, even of Jonah's rebellion; here in this biblical account, God altered Jonah's plans drastically by sending a storm so great that even the seasoned sailors on that ship began to think they were doomed. The ship was going down, yet the men aboard that boat had the insight to know what would save them and that was prayer, calling on the one and only true God whom could save them. That is why the captain of the ship called on Jonah in the storm saying, "What do you mean you sleeper? Arise, call out to your god! Perhaps the god will give a thought to us, that we may not perish." (Jonah 1:6)

Don't be discouraged I say, for when we find ourselves in all our daily circumstances, in the midst of our storms, all we need is to rise and pray to the Lord in our hour of need and like an angel, He will appear and strengthen us. (Luke 22:43; Matt. 4:11; Heb. 1:14)

In another account in the Bible of seasoned sailors about to weather a fierce storm in their lives, Scripture tells us, "And a great windstorm arose, and the waves were breaking into the boat, so that the boat was already filling." (Mark 4:37) As Jesus' disciples, who had observed Jesus pray so much in their journeys together, they felt they had no control of the situation and so cried out to Jesus saying, "Teacher, do you not care that we are perishing?" (Mark 4:38)

The answer to that question is of course He cares; did He not immediately when they called on His name, rebuke the wind and calm the sea? (Mark 4:39) That is what calling on Jesus accomplishes; He stills the storms in our lives, and He may even test our faith in him by stirring up the waters around us that we may go to Him in prayer like we have never prayed before, as though our lives may depend on it. To many that ignore or refuse to pray, perhaps as these sailors thought; Christ is asleep and doesn't care. Perhaps as Jesus slept in the stern of this boat, we may believe, *He cannot be aware of the perils I am facing; no way can He be concerned about my failing marriage, my crumbling finances, my deteriorating health, so regardless of my prayers; how can He be attentive to me and the storms in my life?* Ever give it a thought that maybe Jesus wants us to think this way to test our faith? What storms are raging in your life that you need to get on your knees and call Jesus' name? Oh, but what comfort there is in Scripture to know yet though "I slept, but my heart was awake." (Song of Solomon 5:2)

Truly believe that, though the ship may be tossed, and the sails are battered, I will get down on my knees and beg the Lord to answer me please, to which my Savior will respond, I need not worry, for "Not a hair of your head will perish." (Luke 21:18) "Blessed be the God and Father of our Lord Jesus Christ, the Father of mercies and God of comfort, who comforts us in all our afflictions, so that we may be able to comfort those who are in affliction, with the comfort with which we ourselves are comforted by God." (2 Corinthians 1:4)

My prayer is that you may not fall into temptation, but be delivered from the evil one. (Matthew 6:13) "I love the Lord, because He has heard my voice and my pleas for mercy. Because He inclined His ear to me, therefore I will call on Him as long as I live." (Psalm 116:1-2) The Lord will deliver us from temptation, of this I am sure, for the temptations that we face daily are no different than the ones people of this world have always had to face. But, the only way to endure is by depending on God and His promise that, "No temptation has overtaken you that is not common to man. God is faithful, and He will not let you be tempted beyond your ability, but with the temptation He will also provide the way of escape, that you may be able to endure it." (1 Corinthians 10:13; Daniel 3:17; 2 Peter 2:9)

CHAPTER 3

He Knelt Down And Prayed (Luke 22:41)

————⊷◦⟨∞⟩◦⊶————

"And he withdrew from them about a stone's throw, and knelt down and prayed…" (Luke 22:41) How wonderful it is that we have the Bible as a guide to teach us how to pray. So many times, when we buy new items in our lives such as computers or cars, a large heavy manual of instructions is included with the purchase. How often have I never bothered to consult the manual, but instead set it aside and figure out how things work on my own? Scripture gives us glimpses into the prayer life of Jesus as He withdrew to places of quiet solitude that He may be alone with His Father whom He loved. "You shall love the Lord your God with all your heart and with all your soul

and with all your mind." (Matthew 22:37)
Being alone with our Father, though we may
be surrounded by those willing to see us
perish, is imperative not just for our bodies,
but for our souls. Our instruction manual is
our Bible and yet sadly, many of us just set it
aside, trying to figure things out on our own.

As we observe Stephen, the first martyr,
we have the privilege of seeing in the Bible
that as he was being stoned to death, (Acts
7:60) he committed his spirit to the Lord
while praying for his enemies, bowing
his knees before the Father, knowing that
is where he would find and receive spiritual strength in the face of his tormentors.
As we read of this account in the Bible, it
should encourage us to emulate our Lord
and Savior's prayer life in this hostile world
in which we live.

Jesus arose early in the morning, "While
it was still dark." (Mark 1:35), and, this
became His habit, all so that He could spend
that quality time in conversation with His
Father. The world all but wants to elimi-
nate and violently rip this communion with
our Father in Heaven from our lives, and
we must zealously guard that special time
with all the energy and desire we can muster.
Jesus prayed, asking His Father for wisdom

and guidance in His earthly ministry, even praying for His enemies, as well as for the strength and protection of His disciples and for all believers. (John 17:11)

Jesus knew that although He would be leaving this earth soon, He prayed His Father would watch out for those the Father had given Him promising not to leave us as orphans. (John 14:18) His disciples were to do all He had done and more, (John 14:12) but worse, face all the same hostilities the world had heaped on Him as well. "If the world hates you, know that it has hated me before it hated you." (John 15:18). This verse alone should prompt us even more, stirring a sense of urgency within us to be on our knees that we may be able to endure the world's hatred toward those chosen by Him. Believers are in a dark world, yet with the promise that, "He has delivered us from the domain of darkness and transferred us to the kingdom of His Beloved Son." (Colossians 1:13)

"He has redeemed my soul from going down into the pit, and my life shall look upon the light." (Job 33:28) Yet, how can we live our lives in a twisted and crooked generation as "Lights in the world." (Philippians 2:15; Matthew 5:14, 16; Titus

2:10) By living every waking moment of our lives in a manner "Worthy of the gospel of Christ." (Philippians 1:27) And what does that mean? To live as the Apostle Paul lived, that although he was incarcerated and facing certain death, he lived his life as "A prisoner for the Lord..." (Ephesians 4:1) knowing, "God is faithful, by whom you were called into the fellowship of His Son, Jesus Christ our Lord." (1 Corinthians 1:9)

Can we fully ever know this side of eternity how much time Jesus dedicated to prayer in His short life here on earth? We could get an idea when, in His very own words, He tells us to "Pray without ceasing." (1 Thessalonians 5:17) Does that mean Jesus prayed without ceasing? In the short, frantic life that we have come to know of His ministry, is it a wonder that He ever had time to pray at all. He was popular, He was followed, He was watched, yet He always found time to pray. Jesus, the man, knew He couldn't do it on His own and the only way for Him to accomplish His mission of "Seeking and saving the lost." (Luke 19:10), was to stay as close to His Father as He could and that was by never neglecting His prayer life.

We can be sure Jesus accomplished His goals on both fronts because He confirms it in Scripture when He says to His Father, "I glorified you on earth, having accomplished the work that you gave me to do." (John 17:4) This work the Father gave Him to do can only have been realized by the intimate, quiet times He spent alone with His Father, and that line of communication never went quiet. Instructions from the Father to the Son could not have been transmitted, let alone received, had Jesus not been continuously on His knees. As a result, because of this communion with His Heavenly Father, Jesus completed all with which He was tasked. This most divine link did not go unnoticed by His disciples who were by His side constantly, suspecting at some point in their learning that there was a definite relationship between His power, authority, and prayer life. Certainly, Nicodemus knew or suspected there was a connection as he uttered these words, "Rabbi, we know that you are a teacher come from God, for no one can do these signs that you do unless God is with Him." (John 3:2)[12]

If not for prayer, Jesus couldn't do the things He did, and if we wish to emulate our Lord and do the things He did and

---

[12] Acts 10:38; John 5:36; 9:33; Acts 2:22.

greater, (John 14:12) then we must want to
know everything He knew and do everything He did, including prayer. Our actions
and our words should impact people so that
their lives are forever changed. "For I have
given you an example, that you also should
do just as I have done to you." (John 13:15)
His disciples knew they had to learn from
their teacher if they were going to make a
difference in this world. That is why when
it finally dawned on them that there had to
be a correlation between the things their
teacher did and His prayer life, that they
knew finally where their most important
lesson was going to be, and so they asked
Jesus, "Lord, teach us to pray." (Luke 11:1)

Jesus' disciples had to have been
impressed with His prayer life and I can
only wonder why Jesus didn't teach them
this most vital lesson before they asked
Him. Perhaps this is a beautiful message for
us to learn, that as we have the privilege of
observing Him through His Word at every
crucial part of His life, all along, He has
been teaching "us" how to pray. He prayed
at His baptism, (Luke 3:21) He prayed "all
night" before choosing of His disciples,
(Luke 6:12) He prayed often alone, but
He also prayed when others were around

Him that they may hear Him, such as at the raising of Lazarus from the grave (John 11:42) that we may not only hear but most importantly believe His Father sent Him.

As He miraculously fed the multitudes, (Matthew 14:13-21; John 6) He prayed; in the garden before He was betrayed, He prayed. (Luke 22:40-44) Our Lord and Savior even prayed when He hung on the cross while in agony. (Luke 23:34, 46) There are so many examples in the Bible of Jesus praying that it is as though He purposely left us instructions on not only how to pray, but most importantly, on why we must pray. He was and still is instructing us through His Word, as we pray for the healing of the sick, (James 5:15; Mark 16:18) as we rebuke and cast out demons in His powerful name, (Mark 16:17) as we make important decisions, (Proverbs 2:6, 3:5-6; James 1:5) and as we quite simply, as followers of His Son, wish to communicate with the One who created us. "Call to me and I will answer you, and will tell you great and hidden things that you have not known." (Jer. 33:3) We pray because thank God, He taught us to pray and still is instructing us, His Holy Spirit telling us, "When you pray, say…" (Luke 11:2; Matthew 6:9-13) or "Ask whatever you wish, and it will be done for you." (John 15:7)

In the powerful name of Jesus, we pray if for no other reason than to seek being in His presence! "Seek the Lord and His strength; seek His presence continually." (Psalm 105:4) We pray seeking spiritual strength and "For this reason I bow my knees before the Father." (Ephesians 3:14) Of the many accounts in the Bible of prayer, none specifically instruct us as to what position or posture we should be in, but certainly it is something that, at one time or another, we have wondered. Do I clasp my hands together, do I kneel, do I close my eyes? Suffice it to say, our deportment during this most reverent time when we are communicating with God in Heaven must, however, reflect the attitude of our heart.

When Joshua battled Amalek (Exodus 17:8-16), Moses prayed with his hands outstretched above his head toward the heavens, symbolizing Israel's total and complete dependence on the power of God. Only when his hands wearied, and he lowered them did Joshua experience defeat. Upon Solomon's blessing of the people, (1 Kings 8:54-55) Solomon kneeled in prayer with his hands spread out toward the heavens.

As Jesus prayed and blessed five loaves and
two fish, He looked up to heaven, (Mark
6:41) and before He raised Lazarus from
the dead, (John 11:41-42) He again looked
toward the heavens.

The Bible doesn't specifically guide us
in respect to position, pose, or stance when
communicating with God, but how we pray
and express our deepest emotions and concerns to the Lord will indicate where our
hearts truly are. How much time do we
spend on our knees or even sitting in a
chair looking up to the heavens in total surrender and complete dependence on God?
"Blessed are the poor in spirit, for theirs is
the kingdom of heaven." (Matthew 5:3)

Oh, how I pray with all my soul that
"The Spirit of the Lord God is upon me,
because the Lord has anointed me to bring
good news to the poor." (Isaiah 61:1; Psalm
45:7) As we pray, may the Lord look upon
us with favor, that He may see "He who
is humble and contrite in spirit and trem-
bles at His Word." (Isaiah 66:2) Whether
we lay prostrate before God or kneel, bow,
stand, sit, outstretch our arms, or look up to
heaven, of one thing we must be supremely
confident, and it is that as we pray, our joy
must be complete and absolute in God's

faithfulness to answer our prayers. "And this is the confidence that we have toward Him, that if we ask anything according to His will He hears us." (1 John 5:14)

"Until now you have asked nothing in my name. Ask, and you will receive, that your joy may be full." (John 16:24) This prayer confirms our highest priority in life is the need to ask God the Father, in the name of God the Son, through the power of God the Holy Spirit for whatever we need to accomplish His will, that it shall be done. Then you will know answered prayer brings complete joy. (John 15:11, 16:22) It is in the powerful name of Jesus that we pray, that the Son may bring glory to God just as the Father has glorified the Son. (John 17:1)

Our posture therefore should be secondary to how we prepare our hearts in humility and boldness so as we "Then with confidence draw near to the throne of grace, that we may receive mercy and find grace to help in time of need." (Hebrews 4:16) Whether in difficulty and need or abundance and plenty, our deepest desire and highest priority in our relationship to God as His children must be not to "Sin against the Lord by ceasing to pray." (1 Samuel 12:23) Instead, we must trust God to meet our needs, (Philippians 4:11-13) learning to be content whatever the circumstances, knowing that as we pray, He is but a stone's throw away from us always. In fact, He was there walking by our side all the time. (Luke 24:13-35)

CHAPTER 4

Remove This Cup From Me (Luke 22:42)

⊷∘⬳∘⊶

" S aying, 'Father, if you are willing, remove this cup from me. Nevertheless, not my will, but yours, be done.'" (Luke 22:42) What was this "cup" Jesus referred to in his prayer in the garden that night that brought Him such anguish and despair? Better yet, what bitterness and pain did this cup contain that Jesus the man desired to avoid it all together? When the mother of James and John requested of Jesus that He grant her sons places of favor in His kingdom, (Matthew 20:20) Jesus knew they were thinking of an earthly kingdom. Jesus also knew, this request could only be granted by the Father, (Matt. 20:23) and, aside from positions of honor,

power, and favor, most importantly, what
Jesus was really asking was, "Are you able
to drink the cup that I am to drink?" (Matt.
20:22) When His disciples replied "Yes, we
are able." (Matt. 22:22b), Jesus knew how
true and prophetic their response was, even
unbeknownst to them at that moment that
their own trials would come as they would
indeed share His cup of suffering in their
own cruel deaths. James' demise came at
the hands of Herod Agrippa, (Acts 12:1-2)
and although we do not know exactly how
the apostles died for their faith, Peter, we
understand according to church tradition,
was crucified upside-down, deeming himself not worthy of dying in the same manner
of his Lord, perhaps because of his denial
of Him. (Matthew 26:33-35, 69-75) Though
the Apostle John did not die a martyr, he
lived the martyr's life of suffering, sorrow,
and misery as we know he was exiled to the
Greek island of Patmos during the reign of
terror of Emperor Domitian, and all for the
crime of proclaiming the risen Jesus Christ.
Thank God that in His providential way,
although He allowed John to be banished
this way, it was all to allow him through
the guidance of the Holy Spirit to write the
last book of the Bible. (2 Peter 1:20-21; 2

Timothy 3:16) John was indeed in Patmos to do the will of the Father, "On account of the Word of God and the testimony of Jesus." (Revelation 1:9)

There is no doubt as Scripture tells us, the disciples would drink a cup of suffering too, but their cup would be quite different indeed from the cup Jesus would have to drink. Jesus' cup would be one filled with God's anger and wrath, a cup that was full to the brim and overflowing with all types of heinous sins committed by mankind from murder, to adultery, to all that angers God. "Or do you not know that the unrighteous will not inherit the kingdom of God? Do not be deceived: neither the sexually immoral, nor idolaters, nor adulterers, nor men who practice homosexuality, nor thieves, nor drunkards, nor revilers, nor swindlers will inherit the kingdom of God." (1 Corinthians 6:9-10) And, this is the damning part of this Scripture, as it reminds us, "And such were some of you." (1 Cor. 6:11a) Thanks be to God in His mercy, compassion, and forgiveness, "But you were washed, you were sanctified, you were justified in the name of the Lord Jesus Christ and by the Spirit of God." (1 Cor. 11b)

We deserved to be punished, Scripture tells us, "For the wages of sin is death." (Romans 6:23) But, in His infinite love for us, Jesus offered to drink the cup of God's wrath for us, that His Father's righteous anger toward us would be quelled and we may be saved, not because of anything we have done, but according to His own mercy. (Titus 3:5) As a result, we don't get God's wrath, which we rightly deserved, but His sweet and satisfying eternal love through fellowship in Jesus Christ and His Holy Spirit that lives in us. It was God's will to crush His Beloved Son, "Allowing Him to be pierced for our transgressions" so that by "His wounds we are healed." (Isaiah 53:5-10)

The evangelists Matthew and Mark wrote that Jesus fell on His face as He prayed there in the garden. (Matthew 26:39; Mark 14:35) Scripture allows us to read and feel how He felt, "My soul is very sorrowful, even unto death."[13] Although He was fully God, He was also fully man and the thought of what waited Him had to have been sheer agony. Imagine knowing with absolute certainty you would soon be mistreated, beaten mercilessly, so much so that your

---

[13] Matthew 26:38; Mark 14:34.

appearance would be "Marred beyond any human semblance, and His form beyond that of the children of mankind."[14] How could it feel to be trampled, crushed, and tortured to the point of disfiguration beyond human recognition?

My soul aches deep down inside every time I think, *He did this all for me. There is nothing good in me, yet He loved me so much that He was willing to die this most horrific death for me,* and, yes, for you. (Romans 5:8) How can we ever comprehend this love God has for us that He sent His one and only begotten Son, (John 3:16) a "Lamb without blemish or spot." (1 Peter 1:19), to die an incomprehensible and unmerited death? I thank God, every day by doing my best to live my life in a manner worthy of the gospel of Christ, (Philippians 1:27) that "His grace toward me was not in vain." (1 Corinthians 15:10)

There is no question Jesus knew what He was doing for the truth that can be found in the Bible. Jesus willingly and voluntarily went to the cross for me. "Greater love has no one than this, that someone lay down His life this for his friends." (John 15:13) What a friend I

---

[14] Isaiah 52:14, 53:2, 3.

have in Jesus that although I deserved to die, He took my place instead, and not begrudgingly, He didn't have to be dragged to the cross. "For this reason the Father loves me, because I lay down my life that I may take it up again. No one takes it from me, but I lay it down of my own accord. I have authority to lay it down, and I have authority to take it up again. This charge I have received from my Father." (John 10:17-18)

This willingness to die for us was motivated by nothing more than a love we may never comprehend in this lifetime, but must somehow grasp that the Son of God loved us so much, He gave Himself for me and for you. (Galatians 2:20) And this love we can rest assured is forever, for "Having loved His own … He loved them unto the end." (John 13:1)

Surely, Christ's love is greater than anyone can ever know or understand, so I pray each day that I "May have strength to comprehend with all the saints what is the breadth and length and height and depth, and to know the love of Christ that surpasses knowledge, that you may be filled with all the fullness of God." (Ephesians 3:18-19)

Jesus prayed fervently that this trial would pass, but He also understood that it must be as His Father had planned, "For I have come down from heaven, not to do my own will but the will of Him who sent me." (John 6:38) The Bible makes it clear as we read in Psalm 75:8 that all the suffering His Son was about to endure was the course the Father had laid before His Son as the way of payment or as we know it, atonement for the sins His people had committed before Him— sin God cannot endure. (Habakkuk 1:13) Jesus was indeed God's plan, the substitutionary atonement of Jesus Christ dying as a substitute for sinners: me and you. Jesus "Bore our sins in His body on the tree, that we might die to sin and live to righteousness. By His wounds you have been healed." (1 Peter 2:24; Isaiah 53:5) God had planned this substitutionary atonement on our behalf from so long ago, (Isaiah 53) so that all who look upon Him, (Numbers 21:8-9) would have life, inner peace, and healing rather than anguish, grief, infirmities, and death. These prophetic words in Isaiah 53 are so clear in its details about the crucifixion that it happened just as it was foretold. "But He was pierced for our transgressions; He was crushed for our iniquities; upon Him was the chastisement that brought us peace, and with His wounds we are healed." (Isaiah

53:5; Romans 4:25; 1 Peter 2:24) Only Jesus could have atoned for our sins and that suffering that He took upon Himself had to culminate at the cross.

Could it be that although it was prophesied, there was but a moment of human weakness in Him that prompted Him to even make this request to have this "Cup" (Luke 22:42) removed from Him, knowing all along this trial must take place? He knew He came, "To give His life as a ransom for many." (Matthew 20:28), to die on the cross, that by His death, He might destroy him who holds the power of death; the devil. (Hebrews 2:14; 1 John 3:8) Knowing it was His Father's will, I believe the matter was settled, if but for a moment in time eternity, Jesus the man felt weak. He knew ultimately that had that bitter cup been removed from Him, all He came to do would have been for naught and the devil would have been victorious. We needed Him for redemption and salvation and thank God, He knew it all providentially, even before creation. But for a moment of weakness, in the scheme of eternity, that human emotion passed and in His godly nature He delighted in doing the will of God, (Psalm 40:7-8) though it meant

being led "Like a lamb to the slaughter."[15]
No more did He open His mouth in objection for what lay ahead, but in utter obedience He delightfully resigned Himself to do His Father's will. And, for this reason He came, to be victorious, to destroy the works of the devil. (1 John 3:8)

Contemplate for a moment, if you will, what a wonderful way it is to pray to our Father in Heaven that although we may be in sorrow, anguish, and despair of eventual and inevitable death because of the fallen world we live in, we may ultimately resign ourselves to obey and trust Him, even in the face of death. Though I may be presently walking through a valley of deep darkness, dreading what lies ahead, I need not fear, "For you are with me."[16]

That is where our prayer life needs to be, especially in those moments of fear, anxiety, or dismay when in our lives we see nothing but disease, decay, and darkness before us. We must be on our knees believing and trusting that He will never leave us nor forsake us, (Hebrews 13:5) but will always comfort us by His presence and protection.

---

[15] Isaiah 53:7.

[16] Psalm 23:4.

"The Lord will keep you from all evil; He will keep your life." (Psalm 121:7)

Joyfully give thanks to the Father as we pray, "He has delivered us from the domain of darkness and transferred us to the kingdom of His Beloved Son, in whom we have redemption, the forgiveness of sins." (Colossians 1:13) Give thanks to the Father from whom comes, "Every good and perfect gift." (James 1:17), including the promise of eternal life that God has given us in His Son.[17] Thank God, every day, that He consumed that cup for us that we may have eternal fellowship with God and a sweet, satisfying, never ending, joyful, triumphant communion with Jesus Christ, through the Holy Spirit.

---

[17] 1 John 5:11; John 10:28; 1 John 2:25.

CHAPTER 5

An Angel From Heaven (Luke 22:43)

—◇◦◎◦◇—

"And there appeared to him an angel from heaven, strengthening him." (Luke 22:43) The Bible makes it clear that Jesus was fully God and fully man, yet He "Did not count equality with God a thing to be grasped, but emptied Himself, by taking on the form of a servant." (Philippians 2:6-7) We can only be left to wonder; did the angel that came from Heaven come to comfort and console Jesus the man or Jesus the second person of the Trinity? Perhaps this verse in Hebrews 2:7[18] gives us a hint, "You made Him for a little while lower than the angels." Here we see the Lord of Lords,

---

[18] Psalm 8:5.

the Creator of this universe and everything in it, under it and above it, (Col. 1:15) but for a moment in time experience what it truly means because of sin, (Romans 6:23) to be separated from God and the agony that would cause. And, all this suffering He took on was for us, that we might through repentance from sin and faith in Him as our Savior and Lord, be forgiven of our sins and be reconciled with God. (2 Cor. 5:17-18)

This sadly enough would not be the last time He would need comforting and strengthening from God His Father as He would cry out from the cross in pain, agony, loneliness, and distress, "My God, my God, why have you forsaken me?" (Mark 15:34; Psalm 22) Did His Father in Heaven but for a moment in time also have overwhelming compassion for the Son He loved, the Son in whom He said, "I am well pleased." (Matthew 3:16) That, although He sent but one angel by His side, He knew all along His Son merited and deserved "Myriads and myriads and thousands of thousands." (Revelation 5:11)

King David, in time of trouble, praised and called on the Lord and God answered him, therefore strengthening him and his faith. (Psalm 138:3) There is no question the angel that came to strengthen Jesus in His time of anguish knew not only who it was he was upholding, but I can only imagine the privilege, prestige, and honor this angel must have experienced merely being in the presence of God Almighty Himself, the creator of all things. (John 1:3)

"By the Word of the Lord, the heavens were made, and by the breath of His mouth all their host."[19] Here was an angel; a creature sustaining his creator (Psalm 148:5), helping Him physically, emotionally, and spiritually for what was soon to come to his Creator. Again, I repeat, what a privilege it must have been for this angel out of millions or even billions that was chosen to fortify the very God incarnate. Could it had been a Seraphim, angels who praise God, (Isaiah 6:3) or a Cherubim, angels who were considered to guard sacred things, (Ezekiel 41:18; Genesis 3:24; 1 Samuel 4:4) or could it have been an Archangel, only two of which are named in the Bible; Michael (1 Thessalonians 4:16; Jude 1:9) and Gabriel, who appears in both the Old Testament and New Testament.[20] One thing we do know;

[19] Psalm 33:6; 1 Corinthians 8:6; Colossians 1:16; Hebrews 1:2.

[20] Daniel 8:15-26, 9:21-27; Luke 1:11-20, 26-38.

legions upon legions of angels could have been summoned to minister to Jesus, all that was needed was His Word. (Matt. 26:53)

We don't know how many angels there are and what it is exactly that they do. This is I believe one of those mysteries of the Bible that will be revealed to us when in heaven, but thanks to Scripture, we are given a glimpse of their comings and goings, ascending and descending.[21] That Jacob in the Old Testament dreams of angels on a stairway extending to Heaven is significant in this passage, for it relates for us foremost that the angels are first ascending this ladder. How wonderful to think, here they are, all around us doing God's work, only to return to Heaven to report to their Creator the actions and affairs of men on earth. These ministering spirits, oh how busy they must be day and night, ascending and descending to and from their appointed service, only ascending to give account, only to descend and execute the mandates of none other than God Himself. "Bless the Lord, O you His angels, you mighty ones who do His Word, obeying the voice of His Word! Bless the

---

[21] Genesis 28:10-12.

Lord, all His hosts, His ministers, who do His will!" (Psalm 103:20-21)

We know angels appear in the Bible from Genesis[22] to Revelation[23] and that a special function of their existence is to serve "Those who are to inherit salvation." (Hebrews 1:14; Matthew 25:34) The Bible also clearly tells us one of their main reasons for existence, if not the primary reason, is to worship God as they call out to one another, "Holy, holy, holy is the Lord of hosts!" (Isaiah 6:3; Hebrews 1:6) and, to do the work of God. A multitude of angels praised Him at His birth, (Luke 2:13) and after He was tempted by the devil, angels came and ministered to Him.[24] They could have been at His false arrest had He desired to command so, "Do you think that I cannot appeal to my Father, and He will at once send me more than twelve legions of angels?"[25]

So, how many angels were available to praise, worship, and minister to Jesus at the garden of Gethsemane? We are told

[22] Genesis 3:24.

[23] Revelation 5:11, 7:1, 8:2, 12:7-10, 14:6, 8, 10, 17-19; 20:1-3.

[24] Matthew 4:11.

[25] Matthew 26:53; 2 Kings 6:17; Daniel 7:10.

in Scripture just one angel was sent to strengthen him, (Luke 22:43) but as we can guess by what we read in Scripture and Revelation 5:11, there could have been millions[26] at His beck and call. In fact, there could be millions upon billions, and I would venture to say one day, when in Heaven, we will know for sure. Was it an archangel or the Angel of the Lord[27] Himself that came to sustain Jesus? The answer to these questions will remain a mystery until the appointed day and time when He will reveal it to us. (Eph. 1:9)

The Bible itself does give us a hint by telling us that the mystery of God is indeed Jesus Christ. "That their hearts may be encouraged, being knit together in love, to reach all the riches of full assurance of understanding and the knowledge of God's mystery, which is Christ, in whom are hidden all the treasures of wisdom and knowledge." (Colossians 2:2-3) Thanks be to God, that the mystery "Which was not made known to the sons of men in other generations as it is now been revealed to His

[26] Daniel 7:10; Hebrews 12:22.

[27] Genesis 16:7-12; 21:17-18; 22:11-18; Exodus 3:2; Judges 2:1-4; 5:23; 6:11-24; 13:3-22; 2 Samuel 24:16; Zechariah 1:12; 3:1; 12:8.

holy apostles and prophets by the Spirit."
(Ephesians 3:5) God has indeed declared it
all to us by His Word, "The mystery hidden
for ages and generations but now revealed
to His saints." (Colossians 1:26)

The Study of Angels (Angelology)
in the Bible is a theological topic that is
fascinating, but in this chapter and verse, I
can only speculate as to why just one angel
came as Jesus prayed in anguish, in terror,
in turmoil. Several times in Scripture[28], we
see angels are at His side and with just one-
word hundreds, thousands, perhaps millions
of angels would have saved Him, but then
where would that have left us? Sure, He was
fully God, but He was also fully man and it
was this humanity in him that cried out to
His Father in heaven, "If you are willing,
remove this cup from me." (Luke 22:42)

It was I believe His unflinching perfect
obedience to His Father that allowed Him
however to ultimately say, "Nevertheless,
not my will, but yours be done." (Luke
22:42; Matthew 6:10) Jesus' obedience
was put to the ultimate test of faith here, yet
thanks be to God, He didn't give up, for as
Scripture reminds us, "The Lord tests the

---

[28] Matthew 25:31, 16:27, 4:11, 26:53; Luke 22:43.

righteous." (Psalm 11:5) and, He endured though He knew God would withdraw from His presence shortly when He would be hanging in the cross drenched with the sins of the world. God had no choice in the matter; He had to turn away, even from His Own Son, "For you are not a God who delights in wickedness; evil may not dwell with you." (Psalm 5:4) Though God may seem far away sometimes and rightly so, for sin is totally detestable to Him, He at times may need to step away from us, if only just to test our faith and our hearts. (2 Chronicles 32:31) After we have endured as Jesus did, then God will be faithful to His promises and "He will command His angels concerning you, to guard you." (Luke 4:10; Psalm 91:11-12; Ex. 23:20)

Though we may not see them, we should not be surprised at how many angels surround us as children of God, prepared and ready at the Lord's command to guard us in all our ways. The notion of angels sitting on everyone's shoulders as some in this world believe, ready at our beck and call, should be clarified Scripturally: "Are they not ministering spirits sent forth for those who will inherit salvation?" (Hebrews 1:14) These angels, it would appear, are here for God's children, His chosen people, sent forth from God's throne to be servants for all those who will inherit salvation. They are not here to serve the lost, those involved in wickedness, evil, lawlessness and unrighteousness, (1 Corinthians 6:9-10) for it is not they who will inherit the kingdom of God, but those that come to Jesus Christ for the forgiveness and deliverance of sins.

Sin is the work of the devil, and angels from God will not come to minister to them that practice iniquity for they that practice wickedness Scripture tell us clearly, "By this it is evident who are children of God, and who are children of the devil: whoever does not practice righteousness is not of God, nor is the one who does not love his brother." (1 John 3:10; John 8:44; Acts 13:10) Scripture further confirms this notion that angels minister to His people as the Bible says, "The angel of the Lord encamps around those who fear Him, and delivers them." (Psalm 34:7)

The Bible tells us there is blessing for everyone who fears the Lord:

"Blessed is everyone who fears the Lord, who walks in his ways! You shall eat the fruit of the labor of your hands; you shall be blessed, and it shall be well with you. Your wife will be like a fruitful vine within your house; your children will be like olive shoots around your table. Behold, thus shall the man be blessed who fears the Lord." (Psalm 128:1-4)

What wonderful implications this beholds for us in knowing the Lord blesses those who love Him! Christian brothers and sisters, "Do not neglect to show hospitality to strangers, for thereby some have entertained angels unawares." (Hebrews 13:2), and by doing so we may be inviting angels into our homes, our hearts, and into our desperate situations when we may need them the most.

CHAPTER 6

His Sweat Became Like Great Drops Of Blood (Luke 22:44)

————◆◇◆————

" And being in agony he prayed more
earnestly; and his sweat became
like great drops of blood falling down to
the ground." (Luke 22:44) All our prayers
need to be focused on the will of the Father.
Jesus knew the will of His Father was that
those whom the Father gives to the Son will
not suffer a single loss and all will be raised
to life in the resurrection. (John 6:38-39,
40, 44, 54) With this in mind we can understand the responsibility and heavy weight
on His shoulders of the ordeal He was soon
to suffer for that very mission statement. In
order that He may lose not even one, He

knew He had to first undergo being arrested under false pretenses, which He would not protest, for Scripture foretold, "Yet He opened His mouth not." (Isaiah 53:7)

He would be judged in a tribunal that blatantly would disregard any recognized standards of law or justice and, when found guilty, He was then to be subject to a most extreme and barbaric punishment for the nonexistent crimes He was accused of committing. Jesus was to be mercilessly flogged to the point He would be left ripped to shreds, unrecognized as a human being[29] and yet, as though that were not enough, He would then be crucified, a method of slow, agonizing and painful death from exhaustion and asphyxiation after hanging nailed to a large wooden cross for hours, or maybe even days, at a time. The sheer agony Jesus must have been experiencing at the loss of blood and the accompanying hyperventilation and failing organs as He hung dying was then exacerbated by a surmounting dehydration that would cause the Son of God to cry out, "I thirst." (John 19:28; Ps. 69:21)

---

[29] Isaiah 52:14.

How was the Savior of the world responded to at this most simple of human needs? "They gave me poison for food, and for my thirst they gave me sour wine to drink." (Psalm 69:21; Matt.27:48; Luke 23:36; John 19:29) Oh, how I feel in my heart that as He hung on the cross enduring the wrath of His Father in Heaven for taking on the sins of the world, His true thirst was to be restored from the separation of His Beloved Father. "As a deer pants for flowing streams, so pants my soul for you, O God. My soul thirsts for God, for the living God. When shall I come and appear before God?" (Psalm 42:1-2) "O God, you are my God; earnestly I seek you; my soul thirsts for you; my flesh faints for you, as in a dry and weary land where there is no water." (Psalm 63:1) Soon, His Father would indeed quench that thirst for, "Blessed are those who hunger and thirst for righteousness, for they shall be satisfied." (Matthew 5:6). The eternal promise to His Son and to us would be, "Whoever drinks of the water that I shall give him shall never thirst; but the water that I shall give him shall become in him a well of water springing up to eternal life." (John 4:13-14)

There is no doubt that as we read Scripture, as it is related to us in the New

Testament, or foretold in the Old Testament, Jesus was in anguish beyond anything any human being can imagine. His Father's wrath was about to be poured out on Him, a wrath that modern day people may conceive as disturbing or inconceivable, yet as we read the Bible, we know it is a righteous wrath, for God is the same yesterday, today, and forever. (Heb. 13:8) In fact, the Apostle Paul tells us in Romans 2:5, "But because of your hard and impenitent heart you are storing up wrath for yourself on the day of wrath when God's righteous judgment will be revealed." On that day, God will give to each person according to what he or she has done, according to what he or she righteously deserves. But, on that day in the garden as Jesus prayed so must we, that we may indeed have freedom in Christ, (John 8:36) instead of wrath, "For you were called to freedom, brothers." (Galatians 5:13)

The reality and torture of the cross Jesus would endure for you and for me most certainly set in so vividly in His sights, that I am sure it caused Him to pray so intensely that night His body would writhe in pain, His capillaries would burst, and sweat would intermingle with blood which is why Luke said the drops were "like" drops of blood falling to the ground." (Luke 22:44) The King James Version of the Bible in Luke 22:44 says, "And His sweat was as it were great drops of blood falling down to the ground." So, whether it was blood pouring out of his pores or sweat that appeared as blood, either way it is evident from what we read in Scripture that before Jesus endured the torture of the cross, he was already suffering far more than anyone has suffered or ever will.

All this took place before He was even "Hung on the tree." (Acts 5:30; 1 Peter 2:24), for Jesus was fully aware of not only the heinousness of sin, but the destructive nature it heaps on mankind and would soon visit Him with a fierce intensity and weightiness of all the evils of the world attempting to crush the life out of Him all at once. With this realization of impending doom, He still loved us so much that, though this heavy responsibility pondered heavily on His mind, heart and soul, I could imagine that He could not help but wonder, what would happen to those His Father gave to Him if He succumbed. (John 6:39-40)

His mission, the very reason He came down from Heaven was clear and undeniable. It was to do "The will of Him who sent me, that I should lose nothing at all that he has given Me, but raise it up on the last day. For this is the will of my Father, that everyone who looks on the Son and believes in Him should have eternal life, and I will raise him up on the last day."[30] Jesus knew this was a matter of life or death; failure was not an option. Because of our sinful nature, (Romans 5:12; 6:23) and the penalty of sin that we rightly and justly deserve as the pitiful, wretched,[31] and corrupt humans we are, Jesus knew too well that failure to die in our place would have catastrophic eternal consequences. He knew that the wrath God had stored up to give each person as they righteously deserved, instead would be meted out on "His only Son." (John 3:16) God loved "us" so much that "For our sake He made Him to be sin who knew no sin, so that in Him we might become the righteousness of God." (2 Corinthians 5:21)

This is indeed the agony Jesus would have to endure on the cross that He would be willing to "Lay down His life for His friends." (John 15:13), willing to "Show His

---

[30] John 6:39-40, 44, 54; Jn. 10:28, 29; Matt. 18:14; Jn. 17:12; 18:9; Jn. 6:37; Jn. 11:25; 1 Cor. 6:14; Jn. 12:45; 14:17, 19; Jn. 6:27, 54; Jn. 3:15, 16; Jn. 6:27; Jn. 4:14.

[31] Romans 7:24.

love for us in that while we were yet sinners, Christ died for us." (Romans 5:8) It is no wonder that "being in agony He prayed more earnestly; and, "His sweat became like great drops of blood falling down to the ground." (Luke 22:44) The Savior who was "Without sin." (Hebrews 4:15), was about to take on your sins and mine, just as John the Baptist said he would do; "Behold, the Lamb of God, who takes away the sin of the world!" (John 1:29)

That righteousness imputed on us who believe what His sacrifice accomplished for us, (Romans 5:17) must also treasure it as a true gift from God. (Ephesians 2:8-9) Hence, we are no longer slaves to sin (Romans 6:6-7) and bound by death, for the penalty of sin is death, (Romans 6:23) but free to serve Christ as opposed to being in bondage to sin. Freedom in Christ is the only true form of freedom in this world, for "If the Son sets you free, you will be free indeed." (John 8:36) Jesus loved us too much and knew the consequences of our sins were all too real. I know in my heart that Jesus' prayers in the garden that night were not just for Himself (John 17), but most importantly for me and you and for all future believers. What an unimaginable responsibility and weight laid on His shoulders! That is how much God loves us; He knew there was no other way but total sacrifice, which is why His Only Son "Laid down His life for us." (1 John 3:16)

No doubt, Scripture is giving us, but a glimpse of this awesome responsibility Jesus was charged with and no wonder this is the only prayer in all of Scripture that we are aware of where His prayer was so passionate that, "His sweat became like great drops of blood falling down to the ground." (Luke 22:44) Was it truly blood, or was the sweat so thick because of the sheer agony He was experiencing that it was "like" blood. Many a page has been written about this topic as to whether it was blood extruding from His pores, or it appeared to look like blood, so I will not belabor the same point. I will, however, look toward the Bible and how it recounts what Jesus was suffering that night as He prayed. I do believe, however, that whatever emotions He felt as He prayed prior to suffering like no human has suffered or ever will; the pure love of God was on display and what it means to say, "Greater love has no man than this, that someone lay down his life for his friends." (John 15:13)

In my mind, the only way I can try to visualize this intense love is by thinking of a military scenario where the enemy lobs a grenade in the middle of a group and a friend jumps on it to save everyone else's life. Oh, how my Lord and Savior sacrificed it all for me when He went to the cross. He came to save us, but what a heavy price He had to pay to fulfill that goal and truly say to His Father in heaven, "It is finished." (John 19:30) His mission was wonderfully accomplished, the redemptive work for which He came was perfectly complete. He was made sin for us, (2 Corinthians 5:21) suffering the penalty of God's justice, which sin deserved. Was this something that Jesus did begrudgingly, was He ultimately killed by the Romans or the Jews, or a combination thereof?

Always know this as Jesus reassures us; "No one takes it from me, but I lay it down of my own accord. I have authority to lay it down, and I have authority to take it up again. This charge I have received from my Father." (John 10:18) Jesus willingly laid down His life for His sheep. (John 10:10) He gave it all for the sheer joy of our salvation, "Who for the joy that was set before Him endured the cross, despising the shame, and is seated at the right hand of the throne of God." (Hebrews 12:2)

Because of this knowledge that I am in possession of through the Word, that all that awaited me was death, (Romans 6:23) for living such a sinful life, it is this awareness that causes me to come to my Lord so passionately in prayer. It was because of our sins, my sins, that "The Lamb of God, who takes away the sin of the world." (John 1:29), sweat drops of blood because of the agony He had to endure for me and for you. And, it is also why, because of what He did, we are able to live a life of abundance, (John 10:10) not only here, but into eternity. Jesus paid a heavy price that we may live, having to suffer the indignity of His Father in Heaven, turning His face in revulsion as His Son hung on the cross, for Scripture tells us, God cannot look upon sin. His eyes are too pure to see evil. (Habakkuk 1:13; Psalm 5:5; Psalm 11:5) What a heavy price to pay that He would be forsaken by His Father, (Matthew 27:46) that not one person prayed for Him as He hung there all alone, yet this was all a part of His anguish that night, a price He knew He not only had to pay but was willing for "Without the shedding of blood there is no forgiveness of sins." (Hebrews 9:22) Christ suffered, "For our sake He made Him to be sin, who knew no sin, so that in Him we might become the righteousness of God." (2 Corinthians 5:21)

"Christ redeemed us from the curse of the law by becoming a curse for us—for it is written, "Cursed is everyone who is hanged in a tree." (Galatians 3:13) What anguish, alone in the garden, knowing He would soon be torn apart and separated from the love of His Father, a love that had existed even before time itself. Second Peter 1:17 reveals to us that because of what Jesus endured for us, Christ received "Honor and glory from God the Father" and in this verse, the true heart of God for His Son is also revealed when He says, "This is my beloved Son, with whom I am well pleased." (2 Peter 1:17) How then can God forsake Him while He hung on the cross?

My youngest daughter Stephanie asked me one time, "So dad, if Jesus is God and He was praying to God in the garden, then does that mean He was praying to Himself in the garden?" From the mouth of babes, right? Well, all I could think to answer at that moment was yes, God incarnate did pray to the Holy God in Heaven, meaning the only way to God is through God. And how true that turns out to be that Jesus would tell us, "No one comes to the Father but through me." (John 14:6)

There has always been a close relationship with God the Father, God the Son, and God the Holy Spirit, for they have always existed harmoniously as one God. (Gen. 1:26; Matthew 3:16-17; 28:19) This Trinitarian teaching that says God consists of three persons is a doctrine that should not be questioned, but always believed that each of these three persons are equal to the others, almighty, and without beginning. Scripture makes it clear: there is only one God. "I am the first and I am the last; besides me there is no god." (Isaiah 44:6)

We can but only imagine what that brief separation in time of the Father's love cost, but I am certain that the Son's sacrifice can only be described as an indescribable love that simply, on this side of eternity, will always surpass our knowledge and understanding. (Ephesians 3:19; Phil. 4:7) I am amazed at Christ's love for me, which is what leads me to live a thankful and obedient life for what He has done for me, all that through the One who saved us, God may receive the glory.

CHAPTER 7

Sleeping For Sorrow
(Luke 22:45)

———— ∞◦◗◐◦∞ ————

"And when he rose from prayer, he
came to the disciples and found
them sleeping for sorrow…" (Luke 22:45)
All throughout the Gospels, where we have
come to know about the life of Jesus, we
came to see and know our Savior as someone
that was always in control of all He did, to
include His emotions. Yes, there were times
of righteous anger and indignation, such
as when He cleansed the temple of money
changers, (Matthew 21:12-16; Mark 11:15-
18; Luke 19:45-47; John 2:14-16) or when
He angrily called those religious leaders
that were to be taking care of His people
a "Brood of vipers." (Matthew 23:33) Yet,
though capable of being rightfully indignant,

He was also compassionate, sorrowful, and even deeply moved as He wept, (John 11:35) and grieved. Here, at this moment in the garden, when He prayed for life itself (His and ours), we see His passionate focus. It is like an athlete intensely training for the event of his life, working out hard, early hours, long hours, a single-mindedness concentration, yet sadly, the same could not be said for His disciples. Jesus knew where He was heading (John 18:4) and, what He was about to endure on His way there, but sadly the disciples were exhausted even before they took off for the race of their lives. "For you have need of endurance, so that when you have done the will of God you may receive what is promised." (Hebrews 10:36; Luke 21:19; Romans 12:12) The race they were about to run was one that required fortitude, and here they are drained before they could even see the finish line.

The writer of Hebrews as led by the Holy Spirit (2 Peter 1:21; 2 Timothy 3:16) wisely knew to admonish us to "Lay aside every weight and sin which clings so closely, and let us run with endurance the race that is before us, looking to Jesus, the founder and perfecter of our faith." (Hebrews 12:1) We are to run with perseverance, but not before we shed all that clings to us, (Ephesians 4:22) things that can weigh us down,[32] and all that is within us that only pulls us away before we can even make it to the starting line. We have need of this godly endurance, so that when we have done well, then we will "Rejoice in hope, be patient in tribulation, be constant in prayer." (Romans 12:12). We are to be joyful because our hope is Christ; we are to be patient because it is in this life of tribulation and distress that we will learn to be steadfast as we look ahead at that finish line. As Christians, we should be in constant prayer, knowing and believing that it is only through prayer to our Father in Heaven that we will receive strength to run this race, and persevere with wisdom and guidance as we see the finish line. In faithfulness we must devote ourselves to above all, prayer,[33] that spiritual exercise which makes it possible to endure.

How must Jesus have felt when He came to His disciples and found them "Sleeping for sorrow." (Luke 22:45) What did that mean, after all was not Jesus in a state of sorrow and in fact deep distress Himself?

---

[32] Colossians 3:8; James 1:21; 1 Peter 2:1.

[33] 1 Thess. 5:17; Acts 1:14; 2:42; Colossians 4:2.

Here Jesus was in torment, in a state of sheer anxiety, blood seeping out from His pores, and all they could do was sleep. Were they just merely tired because of the late hour of the night, or were they emotionally drained from fear of the unknown, especially at all this talk of betrayal, suffering, and death? (Luke 22:14-23) No one knew better than Jesus Himself what it meant to be human, experiencing the daily demands, difficulties, stresses, and burdens this life places on us. Scripture clearly shows Jesus manifested human traits, for instance we know Jesus wept, (John 11:35) He slept, (Mark 4:35), and He experienced hunger and thirst. (John 4:6-7) Perhaps since He was flesh and blood as we all are, He understood our weaknesses better than we understand them ourselves. Did Jesus then have compassion for His disciples knowing they just couldn't fully comprehend what was to come their way? To ask if Jesus was compassionate, all one must do is read Scripture and see the heart of God the Son has for people in need of any kind. He felt compassion when He saw crowds starving for bread, (Mark 8:2) or when He saw a widow standing by the coffin of her only son. (Luke 7:13) Jesus, no doubt, although it seems He was admonishing His disciples for sleeping, for being weak, for being human, also had sympathy for them. He knew it was for these very reasons that can simply debilitate a human that they were experiencing sorrow, a grief He knew they were soon to fully encounter as He would be led to the cross. So reminiscent of what He would tell us in Matthew 9:36, "When He saw the crowds, He had compassion for them, because they were harassed and helpless, like a sheep without a shepherd."

Jesus the man came to these men, not admonishing them for their humanity but reminding them to stay awake, to be alert as all Christians should and must because the enemy, the devil, the slanderer, our adversary, is vigorously seeking to catch us asleep that he may viciously devour us. (1 Peter 5:8) As the accuser of the saints,[34] do not be deceived into thinking he will pass us by, for he relentlessly seeks the opportunity to but catch us unaware, distracted, preoccupied, all in hopes of defeating any progress we have made spiritually and nullifying any victories we have achieved for the Kingdom of our Lord.[35] "Therefore,

---

[34] Revelation 12:10; Job 1:9; 2:5; Zech. 3:1.

[35] 1 John 5:4-5.

stay awake, for you do not know on what day your Lord is coming." (Matthew 24:42) "Blessed are those servants whom the Master finds awake when He comes." (Luke 12:37)

As servants of the Lord, I stress, we must remain constantly vigilant, working, praying, preparing so that when the bridegroom, the Lamb of God, Christ, (John 1:29) returns in glory, His bride, the body of believers known as the Church, (Matthew 25:1-31) will be spiritually prepared, for His coming will be sudden and unexpected. Endeavor with all your heart and soul not to be caught ill equipped, for those who fail to be ready cannot go to the wedding feast, and will in effect be excluded from the Kingdom of God.

This preparation can best be exemplified in this wonderful parable of the ten virgins, (Matthew 25:1-13) where ten virgins took their lamps to meet the bridegroom. Scripture tells us five were foolish because they took no oil with them, whereas the wise virgins took flasks of oil with their lamps. The foolish virgins became drowsy and slept when the bridegroom was delayed, but upon His return the wise and prepared virgins entered with the bridegroom to the marriage feast and then the door was shut to the unprepared virgins as they heard the bridegroom say, "Truly, I say to you, I do not know you." (Matt. 25:12) Those believers that have placed their faith and trust in Jesus Christ, like the wise virgins (Matthew 25:1-13) in the parable must be watching and waiting for the bridegroom, the King will most assuredly return from Heaven for His bride. "Watch therefore, for you know neither the day nor the hour." (Matt. 25:13) Stay alert, for if prayer is a way of talking to and being in fellowship with God, it is our most sacred duty not to miss out on that most glorious invitation to attend the wedding feast. "Blessed are those who are invited to the marriage supper of the Lamb." (Revelation 19:9)

How then can one communicate one's emotions, desires, and needs and all that's on one's heart and buried deep within one's soul while asleep? Our desire as His children, those who receive Him, who believe in His name, (John 1:12), must be one of nurturing our love for Him while on our knees, continually, "Building yourselves up in your most holy faith and praying in the Holy Spirit, keep yourselves in the love of God, waiting for the mercy of our

Lord Jesus Christ that leads to eternal life."
(Jude 20-21)

This call to persevere in prayer as we
wait for Christ's return is not of our own
merits or promptings, but it is prayer that
can only be accomplished in the power
of the Holy Spirit. (Ephesians 6:18) Jesus
promised His disciples He would come for
them again, (John 14:1-3) so, why be like
His disciples in the garden full of sorrow, for
His promise to them holds true to us today;
"Let not your heart be troubled. Believe in
God; believe also in Me." (John. 14:1) His
promise is that He will come again and
receive us unto Himself. Though one of
the twelve would betray Him, (John 13:21)
though Peter would disown Him three times,
(John 13:38) though Satan was aggres-
sively working to defeat them all, (Luke
22:31-32) though all the disciples would
fall away, (Matthew 26:31) Jesus remains
fast in His promise saying, "I will never will
leave you nor forsake you. (Hebrews 13:5;
2 Corinthians 4:9)

While we patiently wait, we must be
on guard, alert, watching, praying until the
Day of the Lord. "But watch yourselves lest
your hearts be weighed down with dissipa-
tion and drunkenness and cares of this life,

and that day come upon you suddenly like a trap. For it will come upon all who dwell on the face of the whole earth. But stay awake at all times, praying that you may have strength to escape all these things that are going to take place, and to stand before the Son of Man. (Luke 21:34-36)

There is no doubt our daily burdens, struggles, and encounters with danger of all sorts and manners keeps us on edge, exhausting even the strongest of Christians, tempting us to find solutions to our woes in places other than being on our knees. When that happens, and we seek answer elsewhere, as children of God, we sin and unfortunately choose to live with the consequences of our actions. That broken fellowship with God does not have to occur if we but listen to and obey Scripture. "Examine yourselves, to see whether you are in the faith, test yourselves. Or do you not realize this about yourselves, that Jesus Christ is in you? Unless indeed you fail to meet the test!" (2 Corinthians 13:5)

Just as Paul challenged the Philippians to consider their own conduct, (Phil. 1:27) so must we challenge ourselves about our prayer life. Are we praying or are we sleeping? How many hours a day do we sleep, as opposed to pray? Which one is most important: sleep or prayer? Are we even praying at all? These are matters we must each ponder daily and we must consider with the utmost of urgency as we live our lives as children of God. (John 1:12) Is there something more important than prayer that is hindering us from being close to our Father, from feeling the warmth of our Lord and Savior shining bright in the darkest of days? (Matt. 5:16) Jesus wants nothing more than to spend time with us, which is why He is inviting us to Heaven someday that we may spend eternity in His presence and not have to worry anymore. He promises that the concerns, the pains, the sorrows we have in his life will all be wiped away. "He will wipe away every tear from their eyes, and death shall be no more, neither shall there be mourning, nor crying, nor pain anymore, for the former things have passed away." (Revelation 21:4) What then can we possibly argue is more important than practicing the same prayer life of Jesus that we may experience what it feels like to approach God's throne of grace with confidence, "That we may receive mercy and find grace to help in time of need." (Hebrews 4:16)

I would urge you as you read these words, accept His invitation to draw near to Him. "Draw near to God, and He will draw near to you." (James 4:8) What would keep us from putting God first in our lives that through our devotion to prayer we may confidently know the end result soon will be; we shall live with Him forever.

Father, I thank you that I am in your presence through prayer because of what your Son did for me and that it is in His name I am made acceptable to you, forgiven and set free from sin through the Blood He shed for me. I shall forget sorrow as I spend more and more precious time practicing being in your presence. "I love the Lord, because He has heard my voice and my pleas for mercy. Because He inclined His ear to me, therefore I will call on Him as long as I live." (Psalm 116:1-2)

CHAPTER 8

Why Are You Sleeping (Luke 22:46)

———◦◦◦———

"And he said to them, Why are you sleeping? Rise and pray that you may not enter into temptation." (Luke 22:46) This was the second time Jesus had to tell His disciples that they should pray that they may not fall into temptation. (Luke 22:46) The question, however that most gets my attention in this discourse is when He asked them, "Why are you sleeping?" (Lk. 22:46) I ask myself, "Isn't sleep natural to man?" After all, Jesus slept when He was exhausted? (Mark 4:38) How is it He admonished them for such a natural human function of which He Himself experienced as a man? The Bible tells us, He was fully man, (Hebrews 2:5-18) yet fully God, (Titus

2:13) who tells those who are burdened, enduring so much in this sinful and fallen world, "Come to me, all who labor and are heavy laden, and I will give you rest. Take my yoke upon you, and learn from me, for I am gentle and lowly in heart, and you will find rest for your souls. For my yoke is easy, and my burden is light." (Matthew 11:28-30)

We sleep because we need to, but thank God, He "Will neither slumber nor sleep." (Psalm 121:3-4) Instead, He is working while we sleep, and I would dare say confidently and most importantly, when we pray. This verse convinces me that Scripture tells us: "If you abide in me, and my words abide in you, ask whatever you wish, and it will be done for you." (John 15:7) Effective prayer is without any doubt based on faith in Christ and on His Word, that lives in us. Even when our sufferings are too much to bear, and we feel in our emotional, physical, or spiritual weakness we cannot express in words how we feel, the Spirit comforts us from the deepest recesses of our souls as evidenced by the groans from the Holy Spirit deep within us that words cannot express. (Romans 8:26)

No doubt Jesus knew their weaknesses and is not asking His disciples why they were asleep, for He knows better than anyone why we sleep. On the contrary, I believe He was instead telling them emphatically to stay awake spiritually. This command must stir up the need in us, the understanding that, "We must work the works of Him who sent me while it is day; night is coming, when no one can work. As long as I am in the world, I am the light of the world." (John 9:4-5) But, when He would leave this world, which He was soon to do, it was His disciples that would be left behind to shine the light that gives salvation. "You are the light of the world. A city set on a hill cannot be hidden." (Matthew 5:14) And, that light has not throughout the ages been extinguished and, never will. (John 1:5) This light must now shine through us as we walk as "Children of light." (Ephesians 5:8-14), bringing those lost and in the darkness into the light that is the Gospel of Jesus Christ who died for the sins of all those who believe in His name and unconditionally surrender to His authority for "All authority in Heaven and on earth has been given to me." (Matthew 28:18)

Christ knew the nature of the powers of darkness is to overpower the light that is the

Gospel of Jesus Christ Himself, but it is we that will instead resist the darkness with the Word of God and with prayer and we will be victorious! So "Rise and pray that you may not enter into temptation" (Luke 22:46) and desire to give in to sleep, to weakness, to fear, to the desires of the flesh, but instead that you may know the great power of prayer as also experienced by the great Prophet of the Old Testament, Elijah.

The prophet Elijah spurred the people of ancient Israel to make up their minds and either continue sinning and worshiping the impotent gods of their day or return to the true God. But, despite the miraculous wonders Elijah did through God, (1 Kings 18) one thing Scripture tells us is that he was a human being just like you and me. He experienced weakness, doubt, fear, and similar emotions as we do; in fact, the Bible tells us, "Elijah was a man with a nature like ours." (James 5:17-18) But, despite his human frailties, most importantly we read in these verses is that, "He prayed fervently." Elijah faithfully, we read, carried out the work God laid before him to do and, I am convinced the only way he was able to carry out God's mission was because he prayed earnestly, passionately, and persistently. Yes,

Elijah was just an ordinary man because that is what God said of him, (James 5:17) and that is what should encourage us to pray for if he was a man with a human nature just like ours, imagine what we can do, what superhuman, supernatural feats we can accomplish through the power of God if we just get on our knees.

We are living in a time when men and women of God must stand firm and pray with all their hearts for just as the prophet Elijah knew he had to pray fervently to turn his people of ancient Israel from sin and back to God, so must we also be praying and crying out to God for His people of today to return to the One and only true God. "If my people who are called by my name humble themselves, and pray and seek my face and turn from their wicked ways, then I will hear from Heaven and will forgive their sin and heal their land." (2 Chronicles 7:14)

Even though many Christians may consider themselves "spiritual" it is not until we earnestly seek His face and His presence through prayer that He will not hide His face from us but instead answer our righteous prayers. King David sought the protection of the Lord through many an earnest prayer, "O God, save me by your name, and vindicate me by your might. O God, hear my prayer; give ear to the words of my mouth." (Psalm 54:1-2) As David was hotly pursued by Saul or by ungodly men seeking to put an end to his life, so must we be in our many times of anxiety, crying out to God for help for our very lives, confidently trusting in the Lord's abilities for complete deliverance. David asked the Lord not to abandon him in his time of need and just as God instructed David, so is he instructing us to "Seek My face." (Psalm 27:8) In righteous prayer God will not forsake us, but answer when we call on Him. "Ask and it will be given to you; seek, and you will find; knock, and it will be opened to you." (Matthew 7:7) God not only answers our prayers, but welcomes them, urging us to come to Him consistently, persistently asking, seeking, and knocking because our Father in Heaven, I am convinced with all my heart, delights in giving those who persist in prayer, for "Every good gift and every perfect gift is from above." (James 1:17)

Prayer needs to be earnest and tenacious like that of the persistent widow, (Luke 18:1-8) a parable that teaches us that we ought to pray and not lose heart, pray and not give up, continually pleading as the widow did until the unjust judge finally decided to grant her justice. The moral of the parable as Jesus enlightens us (Luke 18: 5-8) is, that if an unjust earthly judge would grant justice, then imagine how much more God the "Righteous Judge" (Ps. 7:11) will give justice quickly to His elect who cry out to Him day and night. (Luke 18:6-8) As the psalmist prayed day and night (Psalm 88:1-2) for deliverance from his terrible afflictions, so shall we be rescued when we pray, for "Salvation belongs to the Lord." (Psalm 3:8; Isaiah 25:9) Half-hearted prayer is self-defeating and impotent, but sincere heartfelt prayer bathed in faith will not only move mountains, (Matthew 17:20) but will move the heart of God as Scripture comforts us in this, "And will not God give justice to His elect, who cry out to Him day and night?" (Luke 18:7) What an encouraging lesson our Lord has taught us, that we should be faithfully praying for it will most assuredly get the attention of "Our Father in heaven." (Matthew 6:9)

How were Jesus' disciples supposed to pray then, so as not to fall into temptation? First, the Bible tells us that we all face temptation, (1 Corinthians 10:13) and that should bring us some comfort, for whatever weaknesses the disciples experienced in the garden that night, so do we face today. And it's not like Jesus is oblivious to this because as a man, He also knew what it was to be tempted. "For we do not have a high priest who is unable to sympathize with our weaknesses, but one who, in every respect has been tempted as we are, yet without sin." (Hebrews 4:15)

Since the fall of man, (Genesis 3) that very temptation to sin lives in us and the devil knows that, so it is he through our sinful nature, (James 1:14) that he entices us to make wrong, sinful, and lustful decisions that lead us into temptation. That is why God gives us the antidote and that is to "Set your minds on things that are above, not on things that are on earth." (Colossians 3:2)

"Watch and pray that you may not enter into temptation. The spirit indeed is willing, but the flesh is weak." (Matthew 26:41) Only then, as we pray, do we come closer to Him and have the mind of Christ, enjoying the full benefits of living a Spirit-led life that can only be accomplished through prayer. Many a Christian may underestimate the power of Satan to tempt them and influence them and make them believe they are acting and even talking like good Christians, for as long as their life is devoid of prayer, the devil knows a non-praying Christian poses no threat to him. The evil one knows you are impotent on your own, but as soon as Christians pray as followers of Christ, the King of Kings and Lord of Lords who dwells in each of us is the One that will empower us to be able to resist the "schemes of the devil" (Ephesians 6:11) and begin living a victorious life for the devil will fully know that by being on our knees the message we will convey powerfully to the enemy is that, "He who is in you is greater that he who is in the world." (1 John 4:4) "What then shall we say to these things? If God is for us, who can be against us?" (Romans 8:31)

Take encouragement from the Bible and ask the Lord in prayer as you deal with the struggles you face each day, that He may strengthen you with the power of His Holy Spirit, "That according to the riches of his glory He may grant you to be strengthened with power through His Spirit in your inner being." (Ephesians 3:16) God's Word promises that we will not be tempted beyond anything we can bear. (1 Cor. 10:13) So, from today forward, trust Jesus, "So we can confidently say, 'The Lord is my helper;

I will not fear; what can man do to me?"
(Hebrews 13:6) "Blessing and glory and
wisdom and thanksgiving and honor and
power and might be to our God forever and
ever! Amen." (Revelation 7:12)

Conclusion

⊷∘⟨✤⟩∘⊶

T he more I read these verses in Luke 22:39-46, the more it started to dawn on me, this was to be Jesus' last time of prayer as a free man while here on earth. Sure, He prayed from the cross as He cried out to His Father, "My God, my God, why have you forsaken me?" (Matthew 27:46; Psalm 22:1), and He prayed for His Father to forgive those that were cruelly killing Him, "Father, forgive them, for they know not what they do." (Luke 23:34)

Yet, here was Jesus, getting away for the last time for some quiet one-on-one time with His Father and we are privileged, thanks to Scripture, to eavesdrop on this intimate conversation between the Father and His Beloved Son. We can now envision how Jesus felt, and how He prayed as His life here on earth as a man was drawing near to an end. I have not heard anyone tell me yet that they finally got it, that they know how to pray, that they have it all figured out, that they know the secret of real deep prayer so much so that I want to pray just like them. The only One I know that got it was Jesus, so much so that His own disciples asked Him, *"Lord, teach us to pray"* (Luke 11:1) a sentiment with which I whole heartedly agree.

Jesus knew what an awesome privilege it was to be able to spend a few minutes with His Father, especially with the busy days He lived while here on earth. It amazes me and convicts me to think how much time we are willing to give to others and ourselves in the pursuit of trivial things, yet, when it comes to the important things, we the Church body fall short so many times especially when the consequences are of an eternal nature. We may dare not take inventory of our daily hours and minutes and how they are spent, lest we may truly need to cry out for forgiveness for such an egregious oversight in our prayer lives. What should matter in our spiritual lives above everything else is being on our knees before God our Creator, our sustainer, our deliverer, our Savior, our everything. *"Blessed be God, because He has not rejected my prayer or removed His steadfast love from me.*" (Psalm 66:20)

From the Garden of Gethsemane[36] where He prayed, Jesus knew He was headed to that cruel Cross on Calvary, His time for departure from this earth was drawing near, yet, before He could go back to Heaven, He had something agonizing to do. He would have to pray like He never prayed before. Jesus knew He was soon to lay down His life for me and for you. (1 John 3:16; John 15:13) And, the more He prayed for what was about to come, the more He agonized about the intense pain of mind and body, a struggle from within so violent it caused Him to pray more "earnestly" to the point that "*His sweat became like great drops of blood falling down to the ground.*" (Luke 22: 44) Being the Son of God, why not just end it all painlessly and quickly?

An appeal to His Father in heaven, and He could have had more than twelve legions of angels by His side. (Matthew 26:53; Daniel

---

[36] Luke recorded in Scripture that this place where Jesus prayed was called the Mount of Olives (Luke 22:39-46). Matthew and Mark refer to it as Gethsemane, which means "Olive Press" (Matthew 26:36-46; Mark 14:32-42) This account of Jesus praying is recorded in the Synoptic Gospels (Matthew, Mark, Luke) but not in the book of John.

7:10) But, consider this; had He taken that route, He would have been saying that sin has no consequences. God clearly warns us in Scripture, "For the wages of sin is death." (Romans 6:23) Being the righteous judge He is, His decision was to save us from this death that is eternal separation from God in hell, in which unbelievers suffer conscious torment forever. (Luke 16:24-25)

"God is a righteous judge, and a God who feels indignation every day." (Psalm 7:10; Nahum 1:2) God is indeed a righteous judge and indignant each day because of the pervasive sin, wickedness, lawlessness, and disobedience He sees. It just simply cannot go unnoticed by Him. "Shall not the Judge of all the earth do what is just?" (Genesis 18:25) So, when it came time for Him to be doing what was right and just in those final moments of His life, Jesus could not let sin defeat His Father's plan, for it was through His death that we would "All" be saved. (John 3:16) Sin separates us from God. "But your iniquities have made a separation between you and God." (Isaiah 59:2)

Thanks be to God in His infinite mercy, compassion, and love for us He allowed His Son to die in our place that we may be reconciled to Him. (Romans 5:10) Christ sacrificed His life; God declared Him righteous, and justly so! Jesus certainly had the power and the authority to exercise His divine prerogative in the garden and reverse all that was about to happen, but then all He did here on earth while with us, or for that matter, why He became flesh in the first place (John 1:14; Phil 2:7; 1 Jn. 4:2) would have been nullified.

Scripture tells us, "For the Son of Man came to seek and save the lost." (Luke 19:10) Such seeking, and saving is why He came and what ultimately brought His Father in Heaven glory. "That I should lose nothing of all that He has given me." (John 6:39) meant failure was not an option. The pressure was on in a most intense way that no one has ever or will ever experience. Thanks be to God, His Son, "Becoming obedient to the point of death." (Philippians 2:8; Hebrews 5:8) said, "Not my will, but yours, be done." (Luke 22:42) "For as by the one man's disobedience the many were made sinners, so by the one man's obedience the many will be made righteous." (Romans 5:19)

Scripture tells us of His miraculous birth, (Matthew 1:18-25; Luke 1:26-38) His perfect sinless life, (1 Peter 2:22; 1 John 3:5) His excruciating suffering and disfigurement, (Isaiah 52:14) His unmerited death for speaking the Truth, (John 18:37) and most importantly His glorious resurrection according to the Scriptures, (1 Corinthians 15:3-4) all so that God's power and character can be displayed for all the world to see and know. Yet, what has captured my attention throughout it all was His profound and undeterred times of prayer and time of communication with His Father in Heaven.

The Bible gives us the privilege of experiencing those intimate times of God the Son with God the Father as though we were right there with them. All the while, Jesus was healing, casting out demons, preaching, and doing signs and wonders, He was on His knees at every opportune time seeking guidance, strength, wisdom, power, and protection from His Father in Heaven. The intense dependence on His Father that an unquestionable obedience required of Him could have only been accomplished while on His knees. Though Jesus was fully human, His life depended on the Holy Spirit and not the flesh. The Bible tells us as Christians we are to walk according to the Spirit of Christ, (Galatians 5:16; Romans 8:5) "Which is Christ in you, the hope of glory."(Colossians 1:27) Sadly, we have it the other way around and depend on the flesh instead forgetting that as children of God, we are to be led by the Spirit of God. (Romans 8:14) In 1 John 2:15-17 we are warned not to love the world or anything in it, for "If anyone loves the world, the love of the Father is not in him."

The world is simply hostile to God, "For the mind that is set in the flesh is hostile to God, for it does not submit to God's law; indeed, it cannot. For those who are in the flesh cannot please God." (Romans 8:7-8) As Christians, we are either on our knees in communion with the Father, Son, and Holy Spirit, or we are in an unholy trinity with the world, the flesh and the devil. (Ephesians 2:2-3) The devil wanted to break that communion that Jesus had in the desert with His Father by offering and tempting Him with the same things he offers and tempts us with today: power, wealth, and satisfaction. (Matthew 4:1-11; Mark 1:12, 13; Luke 4:1-13) The all-consuming and endless efforts of the devil is to thwart God's plan for Jesus as well as for us, but Jesus left us the guidance in Scripture to defeat these attacks in our times of hunger, by fasting and depending on every Word of God. No matter how hard the devil tries to trick, deter, or tempt us to fail, falter, and fall, the devil could never penetrate or impede Jesus' steadfast love for God and not the love of the world. "You shall love the Lord your God with all your heart and with all your soul and with all your mind." (Matthew 22:37; Luke 10:27; Deuteronomy 6:5)

The devil is clever. He knows all our weaknesses, and unlike Jesus, the devil is always trying to catch us at our weakest moment because he knows we are all born with a sinful nature and are prone to sin. (Romans 5:12; 7:18) "For I know that nothing good dwells in me, that is, in my flesh. For I have the desire to do what is right, but not the ability to carry it out. For I do not do the good I want, but the evil I do not want is what I keep doing." (Romans 7:18-19) "What a wretched man I am!" (Romans 7:24) Help me Father to be on my knees totally depending on you that I may do your will and not rebel against you because of my frail and weak human nature.

As I become more reliant on my own prayer life for the ministry I do, for my family, to be in unflinching obedience to Him, and ultimately in victory in all I do for His glory, I have but to look at Scripture and understand I am to be on my knees, communicating with my Father in Heaven, as often as Jesus was. If I am to do the works that He did and greater, (John 14:12) then I must also recognize Jesus could not have done it on His own; He had to rely on God for all He was able to accomplish in His short life of ministry here on earth. Jesus was fully God, but He was also here as a man, He was not exercising His deity, but flourishing in all His sinless and perfect humanity.

If we tap into God's power through prayer by following Jesus' examples and realize, if God the Son needed to talk and be in communion His Father, then it is our duty to follow the examples Jesus left for us in Scripture. Jesus in His humanity was able to carry out His Father's will by keeping in focused, intense and continual prayer. We must follow His example on how to pray, for our lives depend on it. It is written that Jesus did many things, "Were every one of them written, I suppose that the world itself could not contain the books that would be written." (John 21:25) Hyperbole? I dare think not for the Bible assures me, "All things were made through Him, and without Him was not anything made that was made." (John 1:3) Was much prayer and communication with the

Father a necessary element to accomplish all these things? I dare not think otherwise.

It is this intense prayer life of Jesus that I hope I can emulate, that if for a moment in my life I may be transported to higher levels of understanding Him, His deeds, His power, and His wonders. (Psalm 147:5) It is through His exemplary prayer life that I pray I may also attain in this lifetime the understanding to do my Father's will for my life. Is it supernatural? Indeed it is! But when one ponders on the simple and straightforward promises of the Bible, all we need to do is probe the heavens on our knees and what we may encounter will certainly be from out of this world.

"Ask, and it will be given to you; seek, and you will find; knock, and it will be opened to you. For everyone who asks receives, and the one who seeks finds, and to the one who knocks it will be opened." (Matthew 7:7-8) This is an assurance that God welcomes continuous and persistent prayer so that we may be amazed at what He can do for us and through us. How will He reward us for our persistent and fervent prayers? This much I know; "No eye has seen, nor ear heard, nor the heart of man imagined, what God has prepared for those who love Him." (1 Corinthians 2:9)

My mother was a prayer warrior and, if not for her prayers, I truly believe in my heart I would not be here today. I thank God, she taught me how to pray even though for a long time in my life I ignored this powerful privilege of being able to approach with confidence God's throne of grace to receive mercy and find grace to help in my own desperate time of need. (Hebrews 4:16) Let this short booklet be of encouragement for you to pray without ceasing, knowing "The prayer of a righteous person has great power as it is working." (James 5:16) What that means to me and to you is prayer is real, it is powerful, and it is guaranteed to move the hand of He who moves the world.[37] Promise!

---

[37] Spurgeon, Charles. "80 Charles Spurgeon Quotes on Prayer" https://prayer-coach.com/2010/10/04/prayer-quotes-charles-spurgeon.

APPENDIX

Only Through Prayer!

⋯⋯❦⋯⋯

As we embarked on a search for a senior pastor at LCC, immediately I thought about what Christ's disciples experienced when they witnessed the ascension of Christ marking the conclusion of His ministry on earth in His bodily form. When they were told by Jesus not to leave Jerusalem, but stay and wait for the promised Holy Spirit, this most momentous event that would herald in effect the continuing work of Christ that He had started here on earth and would soon now be placed in the hands of His disciples. (Acts 1:1-2)

What struck me most about this exciting time in the literal beginnings of the Church was not only that these chosen apostles would soon be going into the world as witnesses (Acts 1:8; Luke 24:47) to preach repentance and forgiveness of sins in His name, but most importantly, would "do the works that I do; and greater works than these will he do." (John 14:12) Before they did anything because they had not yet received the power of the Holy Spirit, they instead gathered in **prayer**.

"All these with one accord were **devoting themselves to prayer**, together with the women and Mary the mother of Jesus, and His brothers." (Acts 1:14)

Jesus had initially chosen twelve disciples to be His apostles, and as we all know well, one of them (Judas Iscariot) went on to be known as the one who kissed and betrayed Jesus, for which he paid an eternal price indeed. It is then in the search to replace this disciple that they all got together in one accord and devoted themselves to **prayer**.

As the LCC Pastor Search Committee comes together to choose a new senior pastor, it seems not only fitting, but imperative that the committee be of one mind and one accord in prayer, as Christ's disciples believed it "good having come to one accord, to choose men." (Acts 15:25) It wasn't just a man they were praying for, but the one God had already chosen for the job so long ago. As it was prophetically written, "Let another take his office." (Psalm 109:8)

We are seeking that pastor God has already chosen and is presently on his knees praying for this position God has waiting for him. My prayer is that we also fall to our knees and ask God that as He shows us this godly man, through wisdom and discernment and the guidance of the Holy Spirit, that we clearly see him when we meet him in our search.

I have heard some things here and there in my travels throughout LCC about the kind of pastor people would like to see take Dr. Alan Stanford's place, perhaps one that may agree with our programs and ministries or one that preaches this way or that way. This is my charge to the congregation of LCC; get on your knees and do not leave all the work to the pastor search committee, and, as we all unite in one accord, devoting ourselves to prayer, you will know yourselves that when this man of God is shown to us, your prayers will have been just as important as the work of the search committee.

As you do pray, please keep the pastor search committee in your prayers. If you don't pray, you simply will not be a part of the process. Join us in this most important business of taking our church to the next level of excellence as God has already ordained it. We will find as we seek (Matthew 7:7) because prayerfully, if we all depend on God's power through prayer and not in ourselves, this pastor we seek will come to us just as God has ordained it to happen; "only through prayer." (Mark 9:29)

Bibliography

———◦◦◦◦———

Spurgeon, Charles. "Quotes on prayer"
  https://prayer-coach.com/2010/10/04/
  prayer-quotes-charles-spurgeon.

The Holy Bible: English Standard Version.
  (2016). Wheaton, IL: Crossway Bibles.

Yera, John. "Only Through Prayer"
  Leesburgcc.org, last modified November
  22, 2016, http://leesburgcc.org/uploads/
  november_2016.pdf.